MEISSEN PORCELAIN IN COLOR

MEISSEN PORCELAIN IN COLOR

Hugo Morley-Fletcher

Exeter Books
New York

This edition published 1979 by Exeter Books, New York,
under licence from the proprietor Ferndale Editions

Copyright © 1971 Barrie and Jenkins
Distributed by Bookthrift, Inc
New York, New York

All Rights Reserved

ISBN 0 - 89673 - 007 - 7

Library of Congress Number 79-51511

Text set by Yendall & Co. Ltd, London
Printed in Italy by Nuova Grafica Moderna, Verona
Bound in England by Webb Son & Co. Ltd, London

Contents

Acknowledgements

Among the many people and organisations who made photographs and pieces available, apart from those who for reasons of security preferred to remain anonymous, were:

Messrs. Christie, Manson & Woods Ltd., London

Jacob Stodel, London

Kunsthandel R. G. Vater, Frankfurt-am-Main

Messrs. Winifred Williams (Antiques), Eastbourne

At the time the photographs were taken none of the items illustrated was in a public collection. All were made available by private collectors and by antique dealers in Germany, Switzerland, France and Britain, or were photographed when in the hands of my company, Messrs. Christie, Manson & Woods, to whom I am deeply grateful. Among those I would particularly like to thank are Mr. Robert Williams, Mr. Helmut Joseph, Mr. C. W. Harris, Mr. Jacob Stodel, Ars Domi, Zurich, Herr R. G. Vater, Dr. A. Torré and Mr. A. Embden, whose advice and assistance were invaluable. Many thanks are owed, too, to Michael Plomer who took the majority of the photographs, often under far from ideal conditions. Last, but most important I must thank my wife who, whilst producing a child, has also borne with great stoicism the birth pangs of this book.

Preface

The literature of German porcelain in general, and of Meissen in particular, is, for the English-speaking collector, remarkably limited. Of the major monographs on Meissen published in the present century only one was actually written in English. All the rest are, as one would expect, in German. So for the average collector or student without a command of German there is small scope for reading. This book provides some attempt at a history of Meissen porcelain for those to whom German is difficult and those who do not wish to become involved with minute details. The illustrations have been chosen to show as many aspects of the factory's production as possible, although with such a variety as Meissen offers it is only a tithe of what might be shown. No doubt many things have been omitted which should have been represented, but in this my own likes and dislikes have played a part, aided or frustrated by the eternal problem of finding the right object at the right moment.

Introduction

The history of porcelain manufacture in Europe, if the factory at Meissen, near Dresden, had never existed, would be almost unrecognisable. For almost every subsequent development, every factory owes a debt, generally in a fairly large degree, to Meissen. Apart from the short lived production of the Medici factory at Florence in the 1560s, Meissen was the first successful producer of hard-paste or true porcelain in Europe, where for half a century it held undisputed sway. During this period its products, and then those of its offshoots and imitators, destroyed the supremacy of the Oriental porcelains that had hitherto held a virtual monopoly.

In fact the first fifty years of production saw an interesting reversal of ideas. At the beginning the young Meissen factory had to draw on the products of China and Japan for its shapes and designs. However, the factory soon adapted the ideas of the Orient and made a new vernacular of its own, with the eventual result that even Chinese porcelain made for export to Europe copied its style.

The 1720's, 1730's and 1740's saw the factory progressing from one successful idea to another. It was only a political event, entirely divorced from the factory itself, which closed the great opening phase. Frederick the Great defeated Augustus III in the Seven Years War and Meissen was among the casualties. Many of the workmen were removed to Berlin and much of the factory's impetus was lost. Sèvres was to become the dominant power in European porcelain for the next generation.

During this period Meissen carried on, less creatively but still producing large quantities of useful wares. The figures were less spirited and owed more to the neo-classical idiom which was the follower of the Rococo. This era, although highly prolific, made little significant contribution to the development of porcelain and neither enhanced nor diminished the factory's reputation. The products of the 19th century leaned heavily on those that emerged from the factory in the years of its greatest creative successes.

The heritage of Meissen was a varied one. For the actual material and many of the forms used, the pioneers owed an immense debt to the porcelain manufacturers of China and Japan. With this was mingled the influence of contemporary silver and of the prevailing Règence style. Another powerful influence was the work of the wide range of European print-makers from whom the decorators culled many ideas. The impact of these sources is outweighed only by that of the factory's founder and first patron, Augustus the Strong. His personal taste and requirements laid down the lines which its development was to follow until his death in 1734.

It was Augustus who placed his extensive collection of Chinese and Japanese porcelain at the disposal of the factory, to study and copy. It was he, too, who required the elaborate garnitures of vases and the large white figures of animals for his Japanese Palace. In so doing he not only stretched the abilities of the workmen to the limits, but also made unprecedented demands on the material. Rarely in China and Japan were such massive pieces produced, not simply because they required special kilns, but because the contraction of the porcelain in such large masses is extremely difficult to control, even when a constant temperature can be guaranteed. Thus many of the large animals were technically far from perfect.

However, the experience that this undertaking gave the factory modellers was to prove invaluable in the 1730s when they assumed the dominant role in the process of production. This was the last decade of the Baroque, and Meissen porcelain is one of its foremost vehicles.

The influence of Augustus was replaced on his death by that of Count Brühl whose grandiose taste demanded the production of the great services which were to draw out the genius of his master modeller, J. J. Kändler. Kändler in the same period was producing his lively Italian comedy and animal figures and groups. Throughout the 1740s the flood of figure modelling continued, with Kändler now assisted by J. F. Eberlein, P. Reinicke and, on Eberlein's death, F. E. Meyer: but it was an increasingly Rococo spirit that prevailed.

The advent of the Rococo saw the end of what had hitherto been almost a monopoly. The 'arcanum' or secret of porcelain manufacture had escaped from Meissen as early as 1717 when Hunger had carried it to Vienna where the du Paquier factory was operating, although only on a small scale. Another small hard-paste factory had also existed in Venice, run by the Vezzi family, but these were only minor threats to Meissen's supremacy. The establishment of factories at Capodimonte and Doccia in Italy and at Chelsea, Bow, Derby and Worcester in England during the 1740s, menaced some of the factory's richer markets and introduced wholesale copying of Meissen figures and wares. The 1750s in Germany produced five new factories at Höchst, Frankenthal, Berlin, Fürstenberg and Nymphenburg, all of which afforded further competition to Meissen and frequently adopted its ideas and shapes, if not actually employing its erstwhile workmen and artists. In England the influence of Meissen was never greater than during the Seven Years War, when the factory itself was almost at a standstill. In 1755, however, the transfer of the Vincennes factory to Sèvres and the creation of a Royal Monopoly by Louis XV soon replaced this with its own style.

Despite this, much that the factory created has remained among the staple features of European porcelain in the past two centuries. Particularly in England, even after the Sèvres style had overwhelmed the field of decoration, it was on shapes evolved originally at Meissen that this style was displayed; and until the very end of the 18th century much that was produced at Derby was derived from originals made at Meissen.

In the last century the factory followed the general trend towards overelaboration which prevailed all over Europe. Many of its products were backward-looking, if not actually derived directly from earlier models. However, at the same time, in Dresden, Vienna and throughout Germany, many lesser factories, such as those of Wolfsohn and at Sitzendorf and Rudolstadt, worked in what is generically called the Dresden style, leaning heavily on the tradition laid down by the Meissen factory. So even in an era conspicuously devoid of innovation, the influence of the factory remained strong.

Thus, after 1750, the most important function of Meissen was as a prevailing influence. It is in order to appreciate this in its proper perspective that the study of the factory's development can be of interest and value to collectors of European porcelain of every sort. The story outlined in the following chapters is not only the story of Meissen: it is to a large degree the story of European porcelain in its formative years.

The Early Years
at Meissen

The story of Meissen porcelain extends a short way back into the seventeenth century. As early as 1675 we find records of Tschirnhaus experimenting with minerals to establish the nature of true or hard-paste porcelain. By 1694 he had made some progress and was able to send a small sample of porcelain to his friend Leibnitz. His desire to produce porcelain was not the result of mere scientific curiosity. It derived also from his economic theories which were founded on the principle that each country should be self supporting.

In terms of porcelain it was obvious that Europe, let alone Saxony, was showing a considerable trade gap. This was a situation which interested Augustus the Strong, the Elector of Saxony, even more than it did Tschirnhaus. The opening years of the century saw Augustus involved in the expensive war which deprived him for a short time (1702-1709) of the Polish throne and its revenues. However, during this period the establishment of the Meissen factory was drawing nearer.

In early March 1702 Tschirnhaus met the Alchemist Johann Friedrich Böttger in Dresden at the house of the Prince von Fürstenberg. Böttger had hitherto been preoccupied with the search for the Philosopher's Stone and was as yet only twenty years old. His scientific talents were even at this stage in high demand and he spent a great deal of time running away from his would-be employers. In fact he was escaping from Berlin when he first came to Dresden, from where he was only fleetingly to escape during the rest of his career: Augustus the Strong more than once had him escorted firmly back there. Böttger proved too valuable for his own good. A laboratory was built for him in the Albrechtsburg, Augustus's *schloss* at Meissen outside Dresden, where he continued his experiments under Tschirnhaus's direction. No products of their co-operation can be identified with any certainty, although we do know that they experimented with glass and stoneware. By the time of Tschirnhaus's death in October 1708 it would seem that the stoneware was fairly well developed and that white porcelain was also being made. This progress had been assisted by the discovery of deposits of *kaolin* or china clay, which is vital to the manufacture of porcelain, in Saxony.

Within two years of Tschirnhaus's death the factory was firmly established in the Albrechtsburg. Böttger had the assistance of several workmen, including David Köhler and Johann Schuberth. The period between the official foundation of the factory and Böttger's death in 1719 is generally called the 'Böttger' period, and he must be regarded as the dominant figure at this time.

The products of the factory at this date fall into three categories. The first of these, only to be found in the opening years, is the stonewares. These were inspired by the Chinese tea wares from Yi Hsing which were shipped to Europe in large consignments. Stoneware is an extremely hard substance which takes polishing and engraving with the wheel. It was also to be found in England at this date, where it was being developed by the Elers family.

A Böttger red stoneware teapot and cover, with contemporary silver mounts, c. 1715. The shape was probably modelled by C. G. Lucke. The unpolished surface on the similar example still in the Dresden Porcelain Collection is gilt. This form also occurs in Böttger porcelain.
7¼ in. wide.

The wares made in stoneware show most strongly the influence of their immediate Oriental antecedents. In fact some of them are so close to their originals that they might justifiably be mistaken for them. Conversely many Oriental examples, particularly teapots, have been or are attributed to Böttger at Meissen. However, the Böttger pieces in general show a much higher degree of finish than their Oriental counterparts. Some teapots occur with slightly rounded cylindrical bodies, plain loop handles and with polished bodies moulded with Oriental scenes in relief. These scenes are unpolished and were left so in order to provide a better surface for gilding. Others have pear-shaped bodies, with grotesque masks at the base of the spout and with leaves attaching the handle to the body. The finial on the cover is shaped as a vase. This very distinct shape, original to Meissen, is particularly well-suited to decoration and was to be much used in white porcelain later. Another Böttger teapot shape also owes its origins to the Orient. It has a plain, rounded, almost globular body and short spout set at an angle on the shoulder. The handle is also a plain loop. This shape was to persist in Chinese export porcelain until after the middle of the century, but was soon to disappear from the more sophisticated repertoire of Meissen itself.

Many pieces, bowls and vases in particular, are moulded with stiff leaves round the bases. These, as with the moulded teapots, have the relief parts unpolished to take gilding. The design is derived from two parallel sources. It is to be found frequently on the Chinese blue and white porcelain which was available in such large quantities and it also occurs on contemporary silver, although this in turn was probably inspired by

11

Oriental porcelain.

Strongly reminiscent of contemporary silver or often pewter, are the severe plain cylindrical tankards. The surface of these is highly polished and forms a very successful contrast to the rich Dresden or Augsburg silver mounts with which they were embellished. This plain shape was to endure in the white porcelain, as were indeed many of the forms for cream pots, teapots and other wares, although the stoneware material imposed serious limitations on the decoration that could be used. This was either gilding, engraving or polishing or a combination of these three. Faceting, imparting an effect similar to the surface of early cut glass, is also found.

The figures produced in stoneware are even fewer than the wares. Generally these are undecorated, although one or two Italian comedy figures exist with enamel decoration. Unfortunately, little is known about the modellers at the factory in this early period. We do know, however, that in 1709 Böttger was supplied with Chinese porcelain figures to use as models. What these were is fairly easily deduced from the surviving Böttger stoneware and white porcelain copies of Chinese originals. Large figures of the Goddess Kuan-Yin, such as are commonly found in the 17th and 18th century Chinese porcelain, exist both in stoneware and white porcelain. The God Laotse also occurs. Another source, used for medallions such as Wedgwood later produced in England, was German Renaissance ivory work, whilst the Italian and antique sculpture in the Royal Saxon Collection was drawn upon for busts and religious pieces; for instance,

A Böttger red stoneware teapot, 1710–1713, the shape probably modelled by the silversmith Irminger. A smaller but similar example without the sprays of flowers is still at Dresden.
6½ in. wide.

Right
A Böttger red stoneware tankard with contemporary silver mount, 1710–1720. An unpolished example of great simplicity where the surface of the stoneware makes an ideal complement to the silver of the cover. A polished tankard with a stoneware cover is in the Bayerisches Nationalmuseum, Munich, while another may be seen in the Victoria and Albert Museum, London.
9 in. high.

A Böttger red stoneware head of Apollo, 1710–1715. Freely derived from the bronze group of Apollo and Daphne after Gian Lorenzo Bernini's marble original which is in the Dresden Royal Collection. This is one of the factory's earliest recorded models. Another example is in the Germanisches Nationalmuseum, Nuremberg.
4 in. high.

12

the Crucified Christ in the Stuttgart Landesgewerbmuseum which derives from a work of Bernini in Augustus the Strong's collection.

It is not surprising that among the factory's first original figures was one of Augustus the Strong himself. It is not known who modelled this figure, which shows the King in Roman dress and holding a baton, his cloak swept behind him. It is to be found in both stoneware and white porcelain.

The development of the white porcelain body would seem to have taken place slightly after that of the stoneware, although its subsequent use runs parallel to the latter. Almost all the forms to be found in stoneware occur in porcelain, notwithstanding, of course, that the white glazed body offers much wider scope to the decorator. The wares show mainly the same shapes, and the use of stiff leaves continues in the porcelain. Engraved and faceted decoration disappears, but the much more plastic porcelain afforded considerable scope for applied floral relief.

In addition to the shapes already discussed the repertory of the factory

A Böttger porcelain coffee pot and cover, *c.* 1720. A typical example of relief floral moulding. Often found in the white, the rarest pieces are those with coloured decoration.

was almost completely developed in these early years. Hexagonal baluster tea caddies, two handled beaker-shaped cups, plain beakers, tall vases of beaker shape, octagonal sugar basins, deep circular bowls and chamber pots are all to be seen in Böttger porcelain in forms that endure for the next twenty years.

The decoration shows from the start an extensive use of gold. Many pieces, even when having no coloured decoration, have borders of gilt scrolls and strapwork. Others, particularly the pieces with moulded flower sprays, are enriched with enamel colours and gilt scroll decoration together. The difficulties experienced with the firing of the porcelain in this experimental period caused a great number of 'wasters' in the kiln. Many of these, although rejected by the Meissen factory, found their way to outside decorators or *Hausmalers*. A fairly large proportion of Meissen wares suffered this fate and this will be discussed in a later chapter.

The white porcelain figures of this period often occur in the same models as in stoneware. However, the repertoire was gradually expanded. A large series of seated Chinamen was created. These are all variations

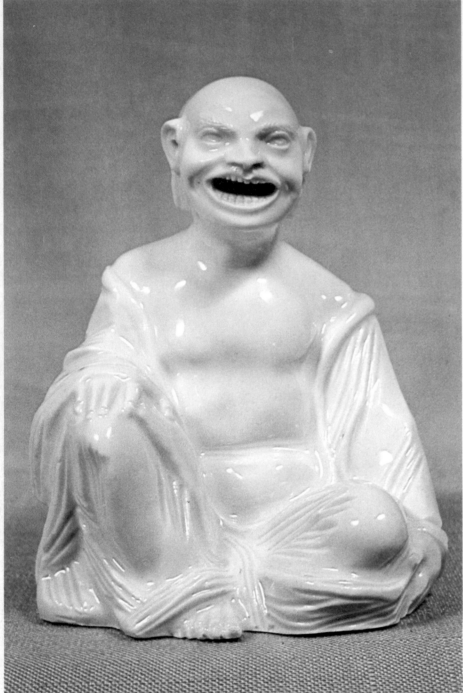

Right

A blue and white double gourd vase, *c.* 1720. The factory records show that by March 1720 David Köhler and Johann Gottfried Mehlhorn had solved the difficult problem of obtaining a satisfactory underglaze blue. Köhler had concentrated on the colour while Mehlhorn had improved the porcelain used with it. Vases of this type were exhibited at Leipzig and Naumburg during 1720. Unfortunately the secret of making this highly successful blue was lost with Köhler's death in April 1723 and the production of blue and white wares at Meissen in later years was very much of a secondary nature. As imitations of the Chinese blue and white vases which were in such demand at the time, these pieces achieved a fair measure of success, though the figures perhaps resemble more closely European magicians than Chinese dignitaries. They are evidence of a very high confidence and technical capacity at the end of the first decade of the factory's life.

20½ in. high.

on the same theme, one to be found equally in early French porcelain at Chantilly. The Böttger figures often have gilt decoration. So too does the range of humorous figures of dwarfs inspired by prints by J. J. Callot.

Owing to the high esteem in which Chinese blue and white porcelain was held, another of Böttger's aims was to imitate this successfully. The factory records reveal the efforts of David Köhler and Johann Melhorn to perfect decoration in blue. Böttger, until his death in 1719, worked hard to produce a good colour, but all the surviving specimens of blue and white wares would seem to date from shortly after his death, or later. In fact it was not until 1720 that the technical problems surrounding the production of blue and white wares seem to have been surmounted: in that year examples were displayed at the Leipzig fair. The surviving vases of this period counterfeit extremely successfully their Chinese prototypes, but retain a certain original quality of their own. Today they are very highly regarded. Yet the production of blue and white porcelain at Meissen was never carried on on a large scale, because the factory was never really satisfied with the colour of the blue produced. (The use of

A Böttger porcelain coloured figure of
Harlequin, *c.* 1720. One of the first and
most successful of the factory's long series
of Italian comedy figures in the Callot
tradition.
7 in. high.

A blue and white tankard, 1720–1725, with pewter cover. Another good example of early Meissen blue and white porcelain with Chinoiserie decoration.

blue underglaze decoration continued on minor wares but does not occur on major pieces.)

The first decade at Meissen was a period of successful experiment. Böttger and his assistants had solved the problem of making a satisfactory body. They had isolated effective enamel colours and gained experience of gilding. Although little progress had been made with figure modelling, which was not to be fully developed until the 1730s, the fundamental shapes were established for the factory's wares. This provided the basis for the great success of the decorators at Meissen in the 1720s. Without the patient development of the Böttger period the flowering of the next decade would not have come about.

Chinoiserie Decoration

In early 1720 Johann Gregor Herold or Höroldt was brought to Meissen by Stöltzel. Born in 1696 at Jena, the son of a tailor, he had worked at Strasbourg and then in early 1718 had gone to Vienna as a tapestry designer. In a few months, however, he transferred to the new factory of Christoph Conrad Hunger, who had left Meissen to establish the first Vienna manufacture in 1717. So he already had some experience of porcelain decoration when he reached Meissen. The manner of decoration he introduced was to consolidate conclusively the factory's success. Under Böttger only one painter is specifically listed among those employed: during the Herold era the number gradually swelled to nearly forty including apprentices.

The style of decoration introduced by Herold was at once typical of the period and extremely original. Broadly, it consists of Chinoiserie scenes within shaped cartouches. The Chinamen appear on terraces, taking tea, smoking pipes and playing with birds on elaborate perches, while a rare piece depicts a lady riding on an elephant. The figures are enclosed by shaped cartouches decorated with strapwork, foliage scrolls and swags of flowers or drapery. During the early years of the decade these were generally painted in iron-red and gold with small panels in lilac lustre, a colour that Böttger had developed and which is often referred to as 'Böttger lustre'. By around 1724 a puce or purple colour joins the palette and by the end of the decade this had ousted the iron-red altogether. On the larger pieces the areas not taken up by the figure panels are occupied by sprays of stylised chrysanthemums in the Japanese manner. These sprays are always described in the factory accounts as *indianische Blümen*. This description distinguishes them from the naturalistic bouquets of European flowers which came in in the late 1730s and which are described as *deutsche Blümen*.

The Chinoiserie decoration on Meissen wares of this period always has a miniature-like quality. It is perhaps best suited to the intimacy of small pieces such as teabowls and saucers, beakers and other smaller wares. When it expands onto large pieces, such as vases and tureens, the technique does not lose its 'minute' quality, in spite of the fact that the figures may indeed be bigger. Usually these figures are depicted full length, although occasionally, as in the service in the Thyssen Collection, Lugano, they are half length, giving an amazingly striking effect.

Of course there was an enormous output of wares of this sort and it would be naïve to suppose that Herold painted them all: the quality of the execution varies markedly whilst the volume alone makes this impos-

Left

A beaker and saucer with landscape decoration; blue enamel crossed swords marks and gilders' letters on each piece. The porcelain dates from the earliest years of the decade but the presence of the enamel crossed swords mark shows that the decoration was executed after the introduction of marks at Meissen. This piece is among the earliest with decoration of this sort, which Herold would seem to have introduced in 1724–1725.

Right

A Böttger porcelain beaker and cover, unmarked. The stiff leaves on this piece are derived from silver and appear also on Meissen stoneware. They were no doubt introduced at Meissen by Irminger. The decoration is another very early attempt at a European subject, though the hand is rather unsophisticated. 7 in. high.

Above
A Chinoiserie beaker and saucer, 1720–1722. This is an extremely early example of the decoration of Johann Gregor Herold, and must surely be regarded as entirely his work. The iron red swag cartouches are typical of the early 1720s, while the tall narrow beaker and the shape of the saucer are also characteristic of this period. The porcelain is unmarked.

Right
A Chinoiserie beaker, *c.* 1725. Here again the debt to the silversmith is obvious in the shape. The particularly delicate Chinoiserie might well be the work of Stadler. 3½ in. high.

Above left
A cream pot and stand, *c.* 1725. The cream pot was one of the factory's staple products, though surprisingly it is not a form imitated elsewhere. Very few specimens have survived with their original stands. The handle is much the same as that found on teapots of the same date.

Below left
A Chinoiserie teapot and cover with blue crossed swords and 'K.P.M.' marks, *c.* 1724. This piece does not differ significantly in shape from the stoneware examples of the previous decade. The decoration of Chinese figures in harbour scenes is enclosed by the more usual *Lauh-und-Bandelwerk* cartouches in iron red, gold and Böttger lustre.
5¼ in. wide.

sible. However, the original conception of every design that occurs was his, although he may well have culled his inspiration from elsewhere. There exists a group of a hundred drawings which are the direct studies for subjects on Herold wares. These were almost certainly used in the same manner as the fresco painter uses a cartoon. The design is pounced through with a pin and traced onto the surface to be decorated. In many cases, therefore, the decoration was carried out by the members of Herold's workshop, and there is strong evidence to suggest that even the work on one piece was divided among several men. There were separate decorators for figures and landscapes, battle scenes and monograms. Another painter specialised in cartouches, whilst others were responsible for decoration in blue and gold, for the ground colours and for painting birds, animals and flowers. Even the simple lines, which adorn the backs of the saucers and surround the panels inside teabowls and bowls, were the responsibility of one artist listed as *Randerer* or line painter. So each piece might well be worked on by four or five people. This extremely 'modern' process is one of the underlying reasons for the consistency of quality of Meissen decoration from the outset.

The decoration, once the vocabulary had been established, did not of course remain static. Besides the pieces with Chinoiserie decoration, which are in the majority, there are to be found a few wares with European genre scenes dating from 1724 or 1725. In about 1726 Herold developed another theme that was to prove as successful as the Chinoiseries; Turkish and European merchants bargaining over bales of merchandise on quays with ships moored alongside. Here again there was great scope for variety. Although this type of decoration was undoubtedly conceived by Johann

25

Gregorius Herold, it is in the 1730s that it is most commonly found and its most proficient exponent was another Herold, Christian Friedrich.

Herold decoration is generally confined to tea wares and vases. Tea services of this period would include a teapot, a coffee pot, a tea caddy, a large bowl, a sugar box and cover, and a number of teabowls and chocolate beakers sometimes sharing saucers. Later services include chocolate pots, hot milk jugs, teapot stands and spoon trays.

The teapots of the early 1720s are usually the same shape as their Böttger predecessors. The coffee pots are of plain pear shape with scroll handles. The tea caddy is at first hexagonal and baluster in shape, providing six most suitable panels for Chinoiserie scenes. Later is becomes rectangular and in the next decade develops an arched shoulder. The bowl is fairly deep for its width and its steep, fairly straight, sides turn out sharply at the rim. Later bowls are much rounder in section. The same applies to early teabowls. The beakers are tall and narrow and saucers are very flat with slightly raised everted borders: in the 1730s the profile is much more rounded. Sugar basins are either oblong octagonal in shape, very low and with knob finials, or they are plain oval with slightly domed covers.

Chinoiserie decoration is also found on small snuff-boxes. The earliest examples are generally of a spreading oval shape. Tankards, too, provide a good plain surface for some of the more ambitious and elaborate scenes. The first tureens also appear in the 1720s. These are fairly simple in form, only the handles showing any plastic qualities. They are closely decorated with small Chinoiseries, whilst the dishes on which they stand provide an ideal surface for the most elaborate scroll work in the prevailing Règence taste. Shaped hexagonal vases, of a pseudo-Chinese shape, flared at the top and rounded below, also occur. These provide an opportunity for rather larger Chinoiserie scenes.

Beside the establishment of a coherent decorative style the early 1720's also saw the adoption of the first porcelain marks at Meissen. The first painted mark, which dates from around 1720, is the *caduceus* or Mercury's staff. This is painted in blue under the glaze. It is not known why it was adopted, although it may have some alchemical significance. It was used only spasmodically and disappeared in the early 1730's. Until autumn 1722 teapots and sugar boxes were marked with the initials M.P.M. (*Meissener Porzellan Manufaktur*) but this was superceded in November of that year by K.P.F. (*Königlich Porzellan Fabrik*, Royal Porcelain factory.) This mark, too, was only shortlived and soon gave way to the initials K.P.M. (*Königlich Porzellan Manufaktur*), which was introduced in April 1723. It very occasionally stands alone, but is generally accompanied by what was to prove the most famous and enduring porcelain mark of all time, the crossed swords—derived from the arms of Saxony. In fact the initials K.P.M. occur only on teapots, sugar boxes and inside small snuff-boxes. On teabowls and saucers the crossed swords appear alone. The early coffee pots, bowls and beakers very frequently bear no mark in underglaze blue. Most tea wares also bear gilt letters or numerals and these are to be found on the undersides of the covers of teapots, coffee pots, tea caddies and sugar boxes. The same number or letter should appear on both base and cover, although two different symbols need not necessarily indicate a marriage. Between 1725 and 1730 the crossed swords mark occurs in addition in overglaze blue. This is because several pieces, which had received their first firing before the mark was introduced, were decorated in this period, and an enamel mark was the only one that could be used in the circumstances. The job of marking the wares fell usually to an unconsidered apprentice, listed in the factory employees as a *Schwerterer* or sword painter. Perhaps as a result the blue crossed swords marks of the 1720's vary considerably. Some have curved hilts and no pommels whilst others have straight hilts and large dots forming their pommels. The marks in overglaze enamels are much more meticulously painted, probably because they were the responsiblity of one of the decorators working on the piece in question. In the 1730's a more consistent style in marking was to be developed.

On pieces for the personal use of Augustus the Strong and on porcelain which he gave as presents, another mark was used. This was the A.R. monogram, signifying *Augustus Rex*, which was introduced in about 1723 and continued to be painted on pieces until 1736. However, many examples bearing this mark must have been decorated at Meissen during the succeeding 15 years. This mark, invariably in a strong underglaze blue, should not be confused with the similar mark, intended to counterfeit it, that was used by Madame Wolfsohn in Dresden in the last century. Mostly it is to be found on sets of large vases for garnitures, which as a result are commonly described as *Augustus Rex* vases. Less commonly it occurs on smaller pieces, such as sugar and snuff-boxes. The pieces bearing the Royal mark are usually richly coloured, although it does appear on a few specimens with underglaze blue decoration. It is to be found on many of the factory's most magnificent, even if not always most beautiful, products.

The style developed by Herold brought to a peak of achievement the decoration of the flat, unmoulded surface of porcelain. It enabled the European porcelain manufacturers to cast off the need to imitate the Oriental originals to which they owed so much. Although decorated with Chinoiserie scenes, Meissen porcelain of the 1720s is essentially European and could not be mistaken for anything else.

Modelling before J.J.Kändler

The modelling at Meissen in the decade after Böttger's death is, of all aspects of the factory's history, the least well documented or clear, although there are one or two facts which stand out and we do know the names of some of the outstanding figure modellers.

One of the limiting factors to the early development of plastic modelling was the difficulty encountered in the firing of the pieces. The wares were much easier to handle in the kiln because they were thinner and therefore less liable to stress cracks. The thicker figures, often modelled from several parts stuck together by the 'repairer', were much more prone to firing cracks and other faults.

The 'Pagoda' or 'Magot' figures of the Böttger period probably continued in production in the next decade, as too did the figures of Augustus the Strong. These last were remodelled in 1728–29 by J. C. Lücke, a modeller about whom little else is known, during his career at Meissen, though he subsequently worked at Vienna where he even signed his work on occasions.

The three dominant names at this stage are Fritzsche, Muller and Kirchner. Of the first two little is positively known. There is a group of figures undoubtedly of this period which might be the work of any one of these modellers. All of them are gauchely modelled and distinctly naïve. They show that the ambitions and ideas of the modellers had not yet been equalled by their technical abilities. However, they also show a considerable understanding of the medium and a grasp of its potential.

Hitherto the plastic products of the factory had been strongly derivative. They had been copied, often without any attempt to alter the models, from Oriental figures or European bronzes or ivories. Only the figure of Augustus the Strong mentioned above and the early Harlequin figures would appear to be original, but the modeller of these is not known. In Muller and Fritzsche, then, we see the first identifiable original modellers of the factory.

The variety of figures that can be attributed to these modellers is not large. Perhaps the most ambitious is a wine barrel or tea urn, intended to stand on a table, supported by four dwarf figures at the angles. Also there are clock cases of almost pyramidal shape with clumsily modelled figures at the sides, and architectural table or mantel ornaments with classical figures in niches. The shape of the clock cases is one found in contemporary pottery stoves but is a new departure in porcelain modelling, which is hardly surprising since the whole idea of a porcelain clock case or watch-stand was an original one. The ornamental group in its classical surround, although not sophisticated in execution, demonstrates very well the ambition and invention of the modellers. The execution is somewhat static because the modellers have not yet really discovered the full potential of their material, and have not realised the necessity for a certain amount of movement.

This criticism applies to a lesser extent to the single figures. For these look forward to the developments in Kändler's work in the next decade. Indeed some of the models anticipate those of the great master. Notable among them is a figure of a seated beggarwoman playing a hurdy gurdy, which reappears in Kändler's œuvre in a more sophisticated version.

Remarkable, too, are the figures of peasant musicians. These highly original conceptions owe no debt to any other art form. They show an incipient movement and vitality which points the way to the great freedom of the following years, and thus are perhaps the most significant creations of these early modellers.

These pioneers made a valuable contribution to the development of figure modelling in porcelain, but their achievement is almost eclipsed by that of the other great modeller of the late 1720s, Johann Gottlieb Kirchner. He was the first man to show an instinctive understanding of porcelain as a plastic material and some of his productions are of outstanding beauty. This unruly and temperamental figure arrived at Meissen in 1727, where he was enrolled on April 29th as a modeller. His stay at the factory was not long and much interrupted by sickness. He also had a rather stormy relationship with his employer, Augustus the Strong.

Kirchner remained at Meissen until March 1733, but for one reason or another was away for considerable periods before this. His most remarkable contributions, although today they may seem rather disappointing, were the large animal figures he modelled for Augustus's Japanese Palace. These, which were of white porcelain, were extremely ambitious undertakings. Even the Chinese potters in the many centuries of their history had wisely avoided unusually large figures owing to the tremendous difficulties in their production. As a result the final products at Meissen generally show some technical defects. They are often heavily fire-cracked, sometimes to such an extent that immediate surgery was required before the pieces could leave the factory. The body used in these massive pieces had to be especially strong to prevent it collapsing in the firing, if not indeed from its own weight. It was therefore rather greyer than the porcelain of the smaller pieces, where strength was a less important consideration. Kirchner's large figures are astounding creations. There was no precedent which the modeller, or indeed the potters, could follow. So from the historical point of view they are of immense interest. However, when compared with what Kändler was to produce in the years to follow, they appear rather static.

Perhaps owing to the severe technical limitations Kirchner's larger figures are fairly simple masses with few significant projections. For instance, the bodies of his animals are supported by their bases or touch the ground directly, and the legs, when not modelled close to the body, rarely play a supporting role. As a result they tend to give a feeling of frozen animation especially when compared with the freedom to be seen in Kändler's figures in the same genre.

Kirchner's smaller figures, however, demonstrate his tremendous understanding of his material. The Neptune he created as the upper part of a table fountain is strongly redolent of the Baroque sculpture of Bernini, but yet a conception which is ideally suited to the medium of porcelain. The subtle shades of surface treatment epitomise Kirchner's awareness of the qualities of porcelain. It looks forward to the use of surface modelling by Kändler and Eberlein in the Swan service, and gives the first warning of the dominance the modellers were to assume in the next decade. In his figure of St Anthony of Padua, conceived, like the large figures and the Neptune, very much as a single mass, Kirchner once again saw the possibilities of porcelain as a vehicle of expression.

Among other figures that may be attributed to Kircher is a small Harlequin figure, his contribution to the Italian comedy tradition. It stands halfway between the Böttger figures of this type and the full flood of the Commedia dell'Arte under Kändler. Compared with the first it is lighthearted and jaunty, but beside the vivacity and imagination of Kändler's figures it is static and unremarkable.

Without knowledge of what was to follow, the achievement of Kirchner at Meissen would seem far greater. His modelling showed the possibilities of the material and revealed its problems when used in large masses. Although overshadowed by Kändler's immensely versatile and confident production, it was Kirchner's work that made this possible.

A white figure of Neptune, 1728–1729, with crossed swords in underglaze blue at the back. One of the most remarkable of Kirchner's creations, this formed the upper part of a table fountain with a large shell-shaped basin below. It is reminiscent of the sculpture of Bernini, and the surface moulding of this figure demonstrates superbly Kirchner's mastery of his material. Complete fountains of this sort are in the Hetjens Museum, Dusseldorf, and another Neptune figure with coloured decoration is in the Bayerisches Nationalmuseum, Munich.
13 in. high.

Left
A spirit barrel and stand, *c.* 1730. Although there are several references in the factory records to the containers for Tea, Coffee, Chocolate and Sugar, it is not absolutely clear who was the modeller responsible. Gottfried Müller in 1725 prepared models of winged dragons and Chinamen as supports for a coffee urn. However, the dumpy little figures at the angles might equally be attributed to Fritzche. A similar example is in the Bayerisches Nationalmuseum, Munich.
7¼ in. high.

Above
A butter dish and cover formed as a tortoise, *c.* 1730, perhaps modelled by Fritzche. Butter dishes formed as tortoises were made for Augustus the Strong from about 1725.
9 in. long.

Right
A figure of a Miner musician, *c.* 1730. Probably modelled by Fritzche, this is one of the earliest of the great series of decorative figures which the factory was to produce, and looks forward to the similar figures modelled by Kändler in the 1740s.
7½ in. high.

The Kakiemon Style

A red dragon pattern plate, *c.* 1735, with blue crossed swords mark. This is taken directly from a Japanese original and is from a service ordered for the Saxon court in 1734 and continuously replaced and increased during the ten years that followed.
9½ in. diameter.

Left
Teawares in the Kakiemon style, *c.* 1730, all with blue crossed swords marks. Here the design is one actually to be found on Japanese porcelain, but the shapes are European, particularly the two handled cups and saucers. The manner in which the shapes and the decoration complement each other is very striking.

Parallel to and contemporary with the wares discussed in the previous chapter, Meissen also produced a large body of wares which were distinctly Oriental in flavour. Augustus the Strong had a large collection of Japanese enamelled porcelains decorated in the manner developed by the Kakiemon family, who had established an individual style in the Arita province in the 17th century, and generally classed as Kakiemon wares. These were housed by the Elector in the Japanese Palace acquired by him in 1717 and specially destined to contain his collection of porcelain. Many of the pieces were made available to the factory to copy and a whole group of Meissen wares was made that followed Japanese originals quite closely. (In fact, examples exist of an exact Meissen copy from a Japanese original.)

The pieces in the Kakiemon style are extremely close to their originals. The Japanese manner of decoration and the forms which typify late 17th century Japanese wares were completely digested by the Meissen potters and decorators. To such an extent indeed did this happen that unmarked specimens are sometimes confused. The Meissen pieces are more rigid

38

A bowl in the Kakiemon style with crossed swords mark in blue. It is decorated with a phoenix perched on pine and prunus branches, and with a chocolate coloured rim such as is usually found on the original Kakiemon wares. Only the shape is un-Japanese in inspiration.
8 in. diameter.

Left

An Augustus Rex bottle, painted by A. F. von Löwenfinck. c. 1728. Blue AR monogram mark. The Japanese origin of the design is quite evident but the brightly coloured palette is alien to it and original to Meissen where the blue enamel colour was evolved by Herold himself. The very white body used for these wares is clearly shown on this piece.
9 in. high.

in form than their originals and the decoration is usually more brilliant and precise.

The Kakiemon originals include octagonal bowls, square sake bottles, chrysanthemum-shaped dishes and hexagonal vases and covers. All these shapes were faithfully copied at Meissen and often occur with the same decoration that characterises the originals. The porcelain used for the wares of this type is quite distinct from that used for those discussed in the previous chapter. It is generally potted much more thickly and the glaze is much whiter than that found on the 'Herold' wares.

In the opinion of some authorities Herold worked in this type of porcelain as well, and there can be no doubt that he was fully conversant with it. He was indeed in charge of the decorators who produced these wares and may well have been influenced by them. However, the breadth of treatment, the scale of the designs and the brilliant palette are essentially different from the extremely original designs with which he is usually associated, and the real masters of this style are A.F. von Löwenfinck and J. E. Stadler.

Johann Stadler arrived at the factory in 1723 or 1724 aged about 22, having previously been employed at the faience factory in Dresden. He appears in the later factory lists as a flower painter and his signed work is indeed flower painting of the finest quality. The painters were not encouraged to sign their work; documentary pieces are therefore rare and very useful in the identification of different styles of decoration, and in associating them with the various decorators active at particular periods.

Adam Friedrich von Löwenfinck joined the factory in 1727 aged about thirteen. He left it some ten years later and was subsequently employed at several faience factories including Bayreuth, Ansbach, Fulda, Höchst, Strasburg and Hagenau. Although through his youth only at Meissen in an apprentice capacity, it would seem that Löwenfinck was allowed to experiment and evolved an individual style of his own. It was fundamentally Japanese in inspiration but includes an imagination and colour which is new. The most unusual contributions are the fabulous beasts which Löwenfinck created. These half-deer, half-dragon or half-horse creatures, painted in dark tones, are shown standing among Kakiemon-type flowers. They are found only on table wares and vases. Similar wares provided the vehicle for Löwenfinck's other most distinctive style. This was derived from Chinoiserie engravings by Petrus Schenk and is epitomised by a Chinoiserie service known as the Jersey Service. The centres of the dishes are richly decorated with Chinoiserie scenes in a palette which, whilst owing an obvious debt to Japanese porcelain, is much more adventurous. The colours are applied in a far broader fashion

than that used in the Herold wares. In both the fable animals and the Chinoiserie services there are gilt suns in the sky. These are regarded by some as a definite indication of Löwenfinck's authorship. However, there are certain pieces, decorated in these two styles, which would appear to have been painted after Löwenfinck had left the factory. So, as in the case of the Herold wares, it might be more reasonable to see in Löwenfinck the originator of these techniques, which were subsequently used by other decorators at the factory.

A lilac ground circular bowl, 1730–1735, with blue crossed swords mark. On this piece the Kakiemon style flowers in the panels are successfully combined with purple *bandelwerk* on a lilac ground. 8 in. diameter.

A sake bottle, *c.* 1730. Copied from Japanese bottles for sake (a strong spirit), these originally had small covers which have rarely survived. Here the comparatively subdued palette is more faithful to the decoration of the Japanese original.

A pink ground beaker and saucer with Kakiemon decoration, c. 1732; blue crossed swords marks on each piece. By the early 1730s the beaker is found either with one or with two handles as in this piece. The pink ground, which appears on the underside of the saucer as well, is a very rare colour and is here combined with an unusually brilliant Kakiemon decoration.

Opposite page
Above
A tureen and cover with circular stand, 1730–1735, with crossed swords marks in underglaze blue. An example of the *Fabeltière* decoration generally associated with Löwenfinck. The slightly raised waved borders are of the pattern called *Neue Ausschnitt* introduced in 1728 and usually found with Kakiemon decoration or naturalistic flowers.
10 in. high and 12½ in. diameter.

Below
Left
A lilac ground tea caddy and cover with animal subjects.

Centre
A gold ground tea caddy with floral decoration.

Right
A blue ground tea caddy with *Hausmaler* decoration.

Three examples of Meissen ground colours on typical pieces of the 1730s. Although the blue ground on the right hand piece was most probably applied at Meissen the figure subjects are the work of the decorator F. J. Mayer of Pressnitz.

Many of the vases supplied for Augustus the Strong's Japanese Palace were decorated in the Kakiemon style. Possibly the earliest pieces bearing the A.R. monogram are blue and white vases copied directly from Japanese originals, but more important to subsequent developments are those with coloured grounds. For it is probably in association with Kakiemon decoration that coloured grounds were first used. These were to prove one of Meissen's most lasting contributions to porcelain decoration in Europe, and, in conjunction with European figure subjects, were increasingly used at the factory throughout the 1730s and 1740s.

In other respects the Kakiemon style at Meissen was rather less influential. It does not contribute so markedly to the mainstream of European ceramics and although very similar wares were produced in England at Chelsea and at Bow, these might equally be derived directly from Japanese originals without the intervention of Meissen. So, although the wares in the Kakiemon style are among those most admired by serious students of Meissen, they are historically perhaps slightly less important.

A brocade pattern plate, c. 1730, with blue crossed swords mark. Derived from Japanese Imari decoration with its rich gilding on shaped blue grounds, wares of this pattern were produced throughout the 1730s. It is frequently described as the 'Warsaw Service'.

A saucer dish, 1720–1723. A very early example of decoration in the Kakiemon style. The porcelain might even have been produced in Böttger's lifetime. The unusual palette includes the rare Böttger lustre and other experimental tones. $8\frac{1}{4}$ in. diameter.

An inkstand with Japanese style decoration in iron red and gold, *c.* 1735. Here a purely European shape is used as a surface for decoration of Oriental inspiration. The shape is reminiscent of contemporary furniture.

A dessert plate, 1735–1740, with blue crossed swords and '22' impressed. The subject is derived from the engravings of Petrus Schenk and the palette used was evolved by Löwenfinck in the Jersey service.

The Work of J. J. Kändler in the 1730s

The departure of Kirchner in 1733 left Augustus's desire for animals for the Japanese Palace unsatisfied. Fortunately for him another master modeller was at hand, Johann Joachim Kändler. It was he, more than any other single person, who was to dictate the form of porcelain figures and wares at Meissen during the next forty years. His ideas during his lifetime were to be plagiarised or adapted by many of the factories that were springing up throughout Germany, France, Italy and England. Hardly a factory is entirely free of his influence, which spread even to the factories of China, where imitations of Meissen were made for export to Europe. In this respect Kändler is a figure of equal importance to the broader development of porcelain manufacture throughout Europe and to the local story at Meissen. Our immediate concern, however, is with the latter.

Born in 1706 near Dresden, Kändler was apprenticed to the sculptor Thomäe in about 1723, and had become a master by 1730. In 1731 he joined Meissen as a modeller and in 1733, on the departure of Kirchner, he was appointed modeller-in-chief. From the start of his career at Meissen his influence grew at the expense of that of Johann Gregor Herold and of the decorators in general.

For the two years that Kändler spent at Meissen with Kirchner, the two modellers worked together on the project dearest to their Elector's heart. As a result when Kirchner left, Kändler was fully versed in the problems and possibilities of the manufacture of the large figures. He also had the benefit of Kirchner's greater experience with the material. In view of this association, the most surprising fact is that Kändler's modelling style is so very different from Kirchner's.

In 1733 Kändler was appointed *Modellmeister* in Kirchner's stead, and continued the production of the animals for the Japanese Palace. At once the difference between his creations and those of his predecessor is evident. Where Kirchner's animals had been static, comparatively lifeless and unrealistic, those of Kändler are full of movement, almost 'alive' and show a very accurate observation of the original animals.

This was made easy for Kändler by another of Augustus the Strong's ruling passions, zoology. The Elector, like many of his colleagues at this time, devoted a great deal of energy to the formation of a menagerie. Between 1730 and 1733 he sent an expedition to Africa to acquire animals for this, whilst his collection also housed numerous stuffed birds. So the opportunity to study both living animals and the more conveniently immobile specimens in the Royal cabinets was an enormous advantage to the modeller. The number of precedents for him to follow was extremely limited. Apart from those created by Kirchner, Kändler's large animals and birds were almost the first in the history of porcelain manufacture. The Chinese had confined the production of figures of this sort to glazed pottery, which was not nearly so difficult to fire. Even then they had not

Left
A large white figure of an Eagle, *c.* 1732. Kirchner modelled an eagle which was extremely static and leant heavily on Japanese prototypes. This version by Kändler shows a close study of the actual eagle, although the pose does to some extent refer back to Kirchner's conception. 36 in. high.

Right
A large white figure of a *Lammergeier*, *c.* 1734. Among the later figures modelled for the Japanese Palace by Kändler this shows great virtuosity in every aspect. The richly modelled surface and the carefully contrived but extremely natural pose anticipate the ingenuity of the great Italian Comedy figures. Five of these figures were modelled at a cost of 95 thalers each. 32 in. high.

attempted figures on such a scale. Kirchner's products were limited by his inexperience with the medium on this scale and by his powers of observation. Only when he took his ideas from prints were his figures really successful: Kändler on the other hand had immense powers of observation and made very good use of the opportunity provided by Augustus to exercise them.

The animals modelled for the Japanese Palace in 1733 and 1734 include a pair of goats, a pelican swallowing a fish, an eagle, a turkey, a cock, a parrot, peacocks, golden pheasants, sheep, leopards and several others. These were all very vigorously modelled, showing great truth to the original animals and at times making immense demands on porcelain as a material. In these figures we see Kändler at his most uncompromising, making little or no concession to the limitations of his medium. This characteristic remains constant throughout his first twenty years at Meissen.

At first some attempts were made to decorate the animals for the Japanese Palace in natural colours. However, the already fire-cracked

Above
A teapot formed as a Monkey, *c.* 1735.
An unusually well decorated example, the
fur markings painted with exceptional
naturalism.
7 in. high.

condition of most of the white figures made this an extremely hazardous undertaking. So after a few attempts they fell back on cold enamel decoration. Perhaps fortunately, this, where it was used, has not withstood the passage of time, and most of the surviving examples of these figures are entirely white. As specimens of undecorated porcelain, relying for effect solely on the modelling, they have an immensely striking effect.

Kändler's animal modelling was happily not long confined to these large and unsympathetic but historically important figures. The death of Augustus the Strong largely ended the work on the Japanese Palace, although it continued more modestly until after 1740. Kändler was thus free to devote himself to modelling on a scale better suited to porcelain and simpler from the technical point of view. Although the production of animal and human figures was concurrent they are best treated separately and we will take the animals first.

The massive power displayed in the white figures for the Japanese Palace makes little preparation for the intimate scale of the majority of the remaining animals that Kändler modelled. Among the earliest pieces of this type are teapots formed as cocks, hens, monkeys and squirrels— typical 'conceits' of which the age was so fond. These are modelled with great fidelity to nature and with the animals' tails conveniently adapted as handles. The colouring is bold and rather more forceful than might perhaps be found in nature. In 1734 Kändler had his first exercise in what was to prove one of his favourite and most successful themes, the pug dog. Not merely were these particularly beloved by Countess Brühl, an important factor, but they had a charm which the modeller caught with great skill. They were a subject to which Kändler was to return repeatedly. The factory records contain frequent mentions of Kändler making models of these animals, and there are fifteen or twenty different varieties either of single figures or of several playing together. Dogs, indeed, provided a source of fascination to Kändler for many years. Besides pugs he modelled spaniels, Dalmatians, whippets and Danish hounds, all in amusing and natural representations.

The bird world also constituted a deep and lasting fund of ideas. In the same years as he was finishing the large animals and birds, Kändler had already begun to produce smaller figures of magpies, woodpeckers, golden orioles and doves. On these early birds the colouring is strong and used in simple masses with much of the porcelain left white.

The late 1730s, when the Swan Service was modelled, also saw numerous individual models of swans. These were made both as additional decorative elements for the service and as figures in their own right. Like the service they are predominantly white, even the bases displaying the most limited use of colour.

Squirrels, monkeys, stags, lions and horses all provided subjects for Kändler's observant commentary. The process continued throughout the 1740s. As well as single animals, groups were made, particularly of hounds pursuing stags and bulls. These last are in a style then fashionable at Electoral courts for rather bloodthirsty hunting groups, and are similar to pieces made at Nymphenburg and Ludwigsburg. Though displaying no small technical and artistic skill, they cannot be described as Kändler's most attractive creations.

The observation of nature displayed in the animal and bird figures, though remarkable and the source of some of Kändler's most beautiful creations, is perhaps less significant a contribution than that shown in his human figures and groups. These were also created with amazing fecundity throughout the 1730s and early 1740s. They represent, when combined with the great services, one of the major developments in the last years of the German Baroque.

The most profound inspiration was provided by the Italian Comedy. This, with its wide range of humorous, sad and sympathetic characters, had been the subject of many prints in the opening years of the century and the themes were well known to the general public. The two-dimensional interpretation of the printmaker, hitherto the dominant vehicle of expression for this theme, was now to take second place to the three-dimensional, brightly-coloured porcelain figures created by Kändler. These were to pave the way for a rash of other variations at other factories throughout Germany, in Italy and in England.

As we have seen, a few Italian Comedy figures had already been produced at Meissen, in Böttger stoneware and in porcelain; and Kirchner just before his departure had also made his contribution to the story: but Kändler is the great master of the Italian Comedy at Meissen.

The most frequently depicted character is Harlequin or Arlecchino, the most endearing of all. He was modelled by Kändler in an unending variety of attitudes, both as a single figure and within groups. The earliest example, a small figure seated on white rock-work playing the bagpipes, gives little indication of what was to follow. Its own claim to fame is perhaps that it is the first of a most remarkable series.

The colouring on these Italian comedy figures during the period 1733–1743 is extremely forceful. Large areas of bright iron-red, black, yellow and other colours are used to accentuate the bold effects of the modelling. These help to impart a feeling of monumentality to the essentially small figures.

After the comparatively faltering start, the full flood of great Harlequins came simultaneously with the creation of the highly modelled services for Count Brühl. The poses in which Kändler imagined this one character alone would suffice to establish his greatness as a modeller. Harlequin is shown bending down, shedding tears, seated holding a jug, his hat extended in his other hand, standing singing, holding a pug dog and winding its tail like the handle of a hurdy-gurdy, and in other boldly conceived attitudes. Apart from these individual studies he appears many times with Columbine, dancing together in a vigorous model of 1744, seated together in a model of the previous year, both in striking attitudes, and in 1740 and 1741 dancing with Columbine and with Columbine and a child.

Columbine in Kändler's world was not always faithful to Harlequin. In 1741 Kändler created one of his most stately and yet lively groups, the Spanish Lovers or Beltrame and Columbine, where the compact position of the figures is contrasted with the width of the panniered skirt of Columbine's Spanish dress. As early as 1736 Kändler had modelled her seated while being courted by the amorous Pantaloon, a charming group with a clever circular movement. In about 1740 another delightful model shows Columbine this time singing to the accompaniment of Scaramouche. Here again the dominant effect of the group is the broad spread of Columbine's skirt. In this respect, the last group, and the Spanish Lovers, both belong to another type generically described as 'crinoline' groups.

Around 1740 Kändler modelled several of these groups. They depict ladies in the crinoline dresses of the period courted by gentlemen and attended by blackamoor servants. One of the most elaborate and notable examples is the Heart seller, which depicts a lady in a crinoline dress, a gentleman, a girl selling hearts, and an attendant blackamoor, whilst another stately group is the so-called 'Augustus III and Countess Kosel'.

While the Italian comedy and crinoline groups constitute the two major categories of Kändler's production, there are many other figures for which he was responsible. Earliest of these is a pair of beggar musicians in tattered dress. This was a theme that had already been explored by his predecessors, but the confidence with which Kändler modelled his interpretation demonstrates his mastery of his material. The colouring of these figures belongs essentially to the 1730s, with a few strong colours boldly used as contrasts to the lovely white of the porcelain. They were followed in 1736 by one of the factory's most influential creations, a group of Tyrolean or Dutch dancers, modelled by the newly arrived J. F. Eberlein, a conception entirely in the round with the two dancing figures giving the model a strong circular movement. This adventurous idea was frequently copied by the English porcelain manufacturers at Chelsea, Bow and Derby

A very large figure of a Pelican swallowing a fish, *c.* 1732. One of Kändler's first animals, probably modelled in co-operation with Kirchner. Six examples were eventually produced at a cost of 204 thalers each. The greyish paste, with its liability to crack in the firing, is clearly shown here. 30 in. wide.

The white figures from the Japanese Palace are not well represented in public collections outside Dresden where many of them still remain, though the Victoria and Albert Museum and the Ashmolean Museum both have figures of goats while five animals are to be seen in the Musée Nationale de la Ceramique, Paris.

The Indiscreet Harlequin, *c.* 1740. This
group, modelled by Kändler, with its
bright colours and exaggerated movement,
epitomises late baroque porcelain modelling.
6½ in. high.

Harlequin and Columbine with a child, late 1730s. Another example is in the Germanisches Museum, Nuremberg. 7¼ in. high.

and more surprisingly occurs in Chinese porcelain made for export to Europe.

Another much repeated model dates from shortly after this. In 1737 Kändler modelled Count Brühl's tailor riding on a goat with the tools of his trade hung from its horns. The original group had no base and was supported on the animal's four legs, a very bold and technically difficult departure. Subsequently this group was produced on an oblong base and reappeared in this guise intermittently until the end of the 19th century. It also was copied at Derby and in English pottery. As a result, what was an original and daring idea had been turned by endless repetition into something banal and commonplace.

Towards the end of the 1730s Kändler was joined by Eberlein and then in 1743 by Peter Reinicke. So he no longer stood alone as the source of all plastic conception at the factory. The year 1740 saw his appointment as controller of the entire modelling staff with all the administrative work that the position implied. This same year, may safely be taken as the end of the Baroque and the definite establishment of the Rococo in porcelain modelling.

The next twenty years were to find Kändler working with Eberlein and Reinicke in the new style, one in which they were perhaps more at home than he. The products of this collaboration, which was the last great creative effort at Meissen, are discussed in another chapter.

What Kändler had achieved in the 1730s was astounding. He had taken a comparatively new material and established it as a serious vehicle for expression. Working virtually without serious precedents he had created a vocabulary on which all subsequent modellers of porcelain throughout Europe were to draw avidly. Even when this is not directly obvious, the debt is nonetheless significant. Unfortunately, perhaps, he was almost too successful, or his imitators and followers were too lazy. So many times have some of his most outstanding creations been copied, both at Meissen and elsewhere (as, indeed, they are to this day), that he tends to be judged in terms of these copies, with the result that the lively invention which originally brought the models about is overlooked.

Another factor here is that of decoration. It seems probable that Kändler himself supervised or laid down the decoration that was applied to his figures and groups. It was evidently an integral part of the conception and in the early years, as we have seen, a limited palette of strong colours was used with great effect. The colours of the Baroque were not those of the Rococo and the models of the 1740s were designed with different decoration in mind. In the 1770s and later the models dating originally from the 1730s were used again with decoration in the taste of the day. The result, which was generally at best insipid, has not served to enhance Kändler's reputation. It is only by an examination of examples produced shortly after the original model was made that we can fully gauge his achievement.

Left
The Scowling Harlequin, *c.* 1740. Another of Kändler's most original interpretations of this theme.
7 in. high.

Right
The Greeting Harlequin, *c.* 1740. One of Kändler's greatest models. The small size of the model is entirely belied by its monumentality. The strong colouring is sparingly used and the white porcelain is permitted to make its contribution to the effect.
6 in. high.

Over page
Left
A large white figure of a Paduan Cock, *c.* 1732. Kändler modelled this in the same year as the pelican, and in this model we see his immense ability as an animal modeller fully displayed. Eight of these birds were produced at a cost of 67 thalers each.
30 in. high.

Right
A large figure of a Turkey, *c.* 1733. Also by Kändler, but a rather more static conception, largely as a result of the nature of the animal itself. The delicate modelling of the feathers looks forward to the subtle surface moulding of the Swan Service.
18 in. high.

Harlequin with a Passglas, modelled by Kändler. The factory records for 1741 clearly describe the creation of this figure. 5 in. high.

Left
The Dutch Dancers, blue crossed swords mark, modelled by Eberlein shortly after his arrival at the factory. It was to prove one of the factory's most copied groups. 6¼ in. high.

Right
A figure of a Jay, *c.* 1740; one of several different studies Kändler modelled of this bird. This shows the white porcelain of the tree stump setting off the clear colours of the bird's plumage. 15 in. high.

Harlequin with a Bird, *c*. 1743. Modelled by Eberlein, this is a rare example of his Italian Comedy modelling.
5 in. high.

The Spanish Lovers, modelled by Kändler in 1741. Although produced considerably later, this example still shows the broad 18th century use of colour, which strongly enhances the dramatic effect. Compare the striking differences between this and the group shown on page 117.
8 in. high.

Above
Two teapots and covers, formed as a Cock and Hen, *c.* 1734, with blue crossed swords marks. An early effort by Kändler to reconcile a natural shape with the functional requirements of a teapot. The strong colouring is similar to that found on the pieces of the Plât de Mènage.
9 in. wide.

Below
A pair of small figures of Swans, *c.* 1747. Created by Kändler some ten years after the Swan Service, these figures on a smaller scale are much lighter in treatment than many of his other animals and birds, and much more rococo in spirit.
5¼ in. high.

The Great Baroque Services

The animals created by J. J. Kändler for Augustus the Strong may appear impressive. However, they pale into insignificance beside the work he was to do for Augustus III and his ministers in the years following Augustus the Strong's death. The vast range of services produced by Kändler in this period entirely recast the physical shape of Meissen's products. It wrested the initiative from the decorators and gave the modeller at last an equal role in the creation of the wares. Hitherto the modeller had merely provided as good a surface as possible on which the decorator could display his virtuosity. Now the modelled surface had decorative qualities in its own right which sometimes reduced the decorator's contribution to a secondary role. In the 1720's the dinner wares had been extremely plain in shape. Even the tureens had the plastic interest confined to the handles and finials, and this was entirely subordinate to the decoration. All this was to be changed by Kändler.

The first service with which Kändler was associated was commissioned by King Adolf Frederick I of Sweden in 1732. The basic forms are still plain and although the borders were lightly moulded with scrolls, the

A coffee pot and cover from the Sulkowsky service, 1735–1738, with crossed swords mark in underglaze blue and decorated with the arms of Alexander Joseph von Sulkowsky and his wife Maria Anna von Stein zu Jettingen. The modeller's role in the design of this piece is much more evident than in the coffee pots of the previous decade and the mask spout almost competes for attention with the coat of arms painted on the side.
7½ in. high.

modelling does not interfere with the fundamental shapes, nor does it attempt to compete with the large coat of arms which forms the principal decorative feature. Thus, although the shallow moulded border was a startling innovation, its impact is considerably reduced. However, it is a signpost to the great developments that were to follow. This service was produced in the same porcelain that the Herold wares were made from, i.e. the same body that had been used from the beginning; but from 1733 the factory used a new felspathic body, which was much more robust and plastic.

The year 1735 saw the next two major services. These were ordered by two men closely associated with Meissen, Johann Christian von Hennicke and Joseph Alexander von Sulkowski. At this time von Hennicke was Vice-director of the factory as well as being one of Augustus III's cabinet ministers. The shapes of the flat pieces of this service, which was painted with coats of arms and small Oriental landscapes, were plain with only the rims moulded. However, the major pieces show much more plastic consciousness. The handles of the tureens were modelled with masks and scrolls, whilst the sides were further enriched with roses in high relief. Even this service is unremarkable when compared with that modelled for Sulkowski.

Graf Sulkowski, a Pole by birth, was a page at the Saxon Court in his youth. In 1731 he was placed in charge of the porcelain at the Japanese Palace, so was thus closely connected with the factory. Subsequently he became the Prime Minister of Saxony. The service modelled for him by Kändler was by far the most elaborate the factory had yet produced. The arms of Sulkowski and his wife, Maria Anna von Stein, beneath a coronet are every bit as magnificent as the Royal arms of Sweden or of Saxony painted on earlier services. While the arms were surrounded by orthodox scattered Japanese flower sprays, the concept of the borders was entirely new. Kändler moulded them in a rich basket-weave or *ozier* pattern: the actual rim of the dishes was waved, while the painted centre of each dish was amply balanced by the undecorated border.

As remarkable, too, were the tureens created for this service. These are of gadrooned oval form, with high domed covers, elaborate scroll feet in the Baroque style and similar scroll handles surmounted by nude female

A sugar bowl and cover from the Sulkowsky service, 1735–1738, with crossed swords mark in underglaze blue. Even more than in the coffee pot the form of this piece dominates the decoration which is virtually restricted to those surfaces left smooth by the modeller. Pieces from this service are in the Victoria and Albert Museum, London and the Reiss Museum, Mannheim.

An oil ewer, salt cellar and mustard pot from the Plât de Mènage, modelled by Kändler in 1737. The rather more violent movement of figures riding on birds is complemented by stronger colouring, while the static figure with the salt cellar is treated in more muted tones.
7 in. high.

busts. Here the painted decoration plays a subordinate role and all is focussed on the lion surmounting the cover and holding a scroll painted with Sulkowski's arms. The central tureen is supported on a shaped stand, itself mounted on four shell and scroll feet in the contemporary Règence taste. The shape owes much to the work of the local silversmiths, and gadrooning is a feature commonly found in silver of the day (the work of Johann Biller at Augsburg is probably the direct antecedent of this piece). However, Kändler, whatever debt he may owe to others, has entirely absorbed the borrowed features and made of them a new vocabulary for porcelain. So successful was he that the Sulkowski tureens appear completely new conceptions. However, the novelty of the service does not end here. It also includes the huge candelabra, each formed as a seated nymph holding four branches, and the candlesticks which, like the tureens, were inspired by the silversmith.

This debt to crafts other than the potter's, traceable still in the Sulkowski service, has quite disappeared in the two remaining great services of the decade, the Swan Service and the Plât de Mènage. These were both modelled for the same man, Heinrich Graf von Brühl, who, after Augustus the Strong, was the factory's greatest patron. His two great services epitomise the Meissen of the 1730s just as the vases created for the Japanese Palace stand for the previous decade. Brühl was the most prominent man in Saxony of his day, and it was he who managed Augustus III's precarious finances and who eventually became his Prime Minister.

The first service, the Plât de Mènage, was began in 1737. In June of that year Kändler produced: 'for His Excellency the Count von Brühl two big drawings for epergnes in the Japanese style, prepared with sugar casters and oil and vinegar bottles, so large that they should seem to be from nature.'

The fundamental inspiration, despite references to the Japanese and 'Indian' styles, is Chinese. Just as the Herold Chinoiserie decoration represents the summit of this type of painting on porcelain, so the Plât de Mènage is probably the greatest and most imaginative plastic exercise in the style. As with the Herold Chinoiseries, the Chinese figures that adorn and form the pieces in the Plât de Mènage are unequivocally European Baroque Chinamen. The centre-piece, or 'epargnie' as Kändler

himself described it, is one of the most remarkable creations ever executed in porcelain. With its angry birds'-mask handles, its sides encrusted with brightly coloured swags, its Chinamen beneath umbrellas, and its finely pierced shell panels, it may, taken by itself, give a garish and excessively *mouvementé* impression. Seen as it should be, which is today virtually impossible, set on its shaped plateau and surrounded by its matching salt cellars, mustard pots and sugar casters, in the centre of a suitably large dining table laden with silver and glass, it would be easier to understand and appreciate.

The brightness and violence of the Plât de Mènage was influenced by the elaborate surroundings of the period between the German Baroque and Rococo. The lesser pieces are much more easily appreciated. They share many of the qualities which are found in Kändler's figure of the same time. The casters are conceived as embracing Chinamen whilst the oil and vinegar bottles are Chinamen riding on cocks. These are much more Rococo in feeling than the centre-piece, and the bright colours and movement are less surprising on the smaller scale. The whole con-

A pair of sugar casters from Count Brühl's Plât de Mènage. Modelled by Kändler towards the end of 1737, these show a fine balance between the white moulded surface and the fairly small areas of strong Baroque colouring.
8 in. high.

A large dish from the Swan Service, c. 1738, with crossed swords mark in underglaze blue. In the flat wares of the Swan Service the modelled white surfaces are dominant, while the coloured decoration and gilding are used sparingly. 15 in. wide.

ception was highly ambitious and original and, in the smaller pieces at least, most successful.

The imagination and virtuosity displayed by Kändler in this work gave him greater confidence for the next service he made for Count Brühl. It resulted in one of the largest dinner services ever produced, numbering over 2000 pieces. The design and production of these took about four years and occupied the talents not merely of Kändler but also of Eberlein. The dominant motif was water, a canting reference to the name Brühl, while the underlying shape of the plates was a shell. In January 1738 we know that Kändler spent three days in Dresden 'in the Natural History cabinets to draw shells for the Swan Service'. Shortly afterwards he produced the model plates, to which the finishing touches were put by Eberlein in September. The moulded surface is of unparalleled originality and beauty. The central field of the dishes, which has no painted decoration, is subtly moulded with swans and storks swimming among bullrushes, and the borders are painted with sparse *indianische Blümen* and with Brühl's arms. The sauce boats for the service, which are shaped as

swans and *putti*, were designed by Kändler (there exists one of his sketches for this piece). However, we also know that, in August 1738, Eberlein 'had modelled a new sauceboat of swan and a child in terracotta'. So perhaps here we have a key to this successful partnership. Eberlein seems to have so well understood Kändler's intentions that his interpretation is entirely in tune with the dishes which Kändler did himself. The central tureens were also apparently modelled by Eberlein. These were surmounted by Galatea riding in triumph on a dolphin beneath an arch of drapery. The sides are moulded with cartouches flanked by swans, whilst mermaids form the handles. The feet are formed as entwined dolphins and infant tritons. Entwined dolphins supporting shells form the salts, whilst infant *putti* embracing support the table candlesticks. These last are the sole pieces in the service which are not original to Kändler or indeed to porcelain. They are very close copies of ormolu examples by Meissonier produced in 1735. These were engraved by Delplace and it is probably from his print that the design was taken. Meissonier was one of the greatest interpreters of the Rococo, and this fact explains why a design lifted wholesale from his œuvre is so completely absorbed in Kändler and Eberlein's work in another material. The Swan Service, although only marginally later than the Plât de Mènage which is overtly Baroque in many features, is over the watershed into the Rococo. The breaking up of the entire surface of each piece with shallow moulding and the much more subtle and playful movement is definitely Rococo in spirit. So too is the very restrained use of colour which leaves the white of the porcelain to do most of the work, enhanced by gilding carefully used. This combination of white set off by gold is frequently found in German rococo interiors.

The Swan Service represents the summit of this type of production. It dates from the same era as Kändler's best figures and groups and represents the end of the period in which Kändler worked on his own. The creation of the service saw the beginning of his collaboration with Eberlein and later on with Ehder. This saw the finish of the independent creations of the master and the start of a school of modellers working in the style which he had formulated, a style which he dominated so completely that, written evidence apart, it is often impossible to distinguish the work of Kändler's pupils from his own.

Decoration in the 1730s

The painted decoration in the third decade at Meissen follows logically on from that of the previous years. The Chinoiserie decoration developed by J. G. Herold was carried on by his relative, Christian Friedrich Herold, in a style more brightly coloured than that of the earlier period. The Chinamen are shown seated among palm trees and are generally larger than those by Johann Gregor. In many instances they are not enclosed by scroll cartouches but are standing on elaborate scroll supports, which often contain small monochrome Chinoiserie panels. Though this decoration is fairly certainly associated with Christian Friedrich, and finds its apogee in the service which he painted for the Prince Archbishop of Cologne in 1735, there is evidence to suggest that Johann Gregor may have originated the style.

The shapes which were used also underwent considerable changes. The teapots became baluster- rather than pear-shaped. Their handles became angular and were moulded with shells and scales which were often picked out in gilding. The bowls which had hitherto been deep and fairly straight sided became shallower and more rounded in section. Sugar basins, instead of being oval or oblong octagonal, became plain circular bowls with almost flat covers. The beaker or chocolate cup, hitherto plain and slender, becomes slightly wider and has two dented handles. The tea bowl, like the larger bowl, is rounder and has a slightly turned out rim, whilst saucers, hitherto shallow and with almost flat rims, become deeper and plainly curved. Tea caddies, which in the previous generation had been hexagonal or sometimes rectangular with cylindrical covers, are more often rectangular with arched shoulders. The covers are domed and, as

A yellow ground two-handled beaker and saucer, with crossed swords mark and gilder's numerals, 1730–1735. A good example of Meissen yellow ground, a rich even colour. The *Laub-und-Bandelwerk* cartouche in iron red and puce shows that this is still fairly early, though it surrounds a definitely European landscape scene which is typical of the 1730s.

with teapots, coffee pots and sugar bowls, the finial is frequently a flower. Besides these old shapes which have been modified, several new pieces join the repertoire of tea, coffee and chocolate wares. Teapots are accompanied by stands, often hexafoil or pentagonal. Spoon trays of pointed oval form also appear, whilst tea and coffee pots are joined by special chocolate pots. These, which were intended to have wooden handles, are cylindrical with scroll spouts set at right angles to the handles, and have flat cylindrical covers which required special metal fittings to keep them on.

By about 1735 Chinoiserie decoration was beginning to take second place to European subjects. As early as 1724 Johann Gregor Herold had painted wares with ships in harbour scenes. Christian Friedrich Herold was to make this type of decoration a dominant theme. His interpretation included Turkish and European merchants bargaining over merchandise and loading it onto ships. Often it is associated with coloured grounds such as also occur on pieces decorated in the Kakiemon style. The most common is perhaps lilac, but yellow, turquoise, dead-leaf brown, lime

Above

A lilac ground armorial bowl with blue crossed swords mark, *c.* 1735. Armorial pieces with coloured grounds are very rare. This specimen combines a gilt interior with the lilac outside. Attributable to B. G. Haüer, this was probably painted for a Venetian client as the scene on the reverse is of a canal-scape. The gilt trellis cartouche is a later feature than the coloured scroll surrounds on the yellow ground beaker.
6½ in. high.

An armorial teacup and saucer, *c.* 1735, with blue crossed mark. A less elaborate example of this type of ware, the whole design relying on the coat of arms in its simple surround.

green, dark blue and iron-red are also found. These are sometimes accompanied by burnished gilding, so that the entire surface of the porcelain is covered in either enamel colour or gilding to such an extent that one of the great qualities of porcelain, its whiteness, is almost entirely lost. This was one of the factors in the great rift between the decorators, who saw the surface of the porcelain as a challenge to their use of colour, and the modellers, led by Kändler, who felt the plastic beauty of the white body and wished to limit the use of coloured decoration.

In the 1730s a thriving trade was done in armorial tea wares, principally for the Venetian nobility, although other noble Italian and German

A tea caddy with miners, 1735–1740. The wares decorated with these mining figures are ascribed, like many of the armorial teawares, to Haüer. Miners were one of Augustus III's ruling passions and a number of pieces were painted for him with these subjects. The royal AR monogram is generally painted on the miners' caps. The rarest pieces of this sort depict Augustus and his Queen visiting the mines.

clients are also identifiable. In fact the *locus classicus* of C. F. Herold's Chinoiserie painting is the armorial service he painted for Clemens August, Archbishop and Elector of Cologne. With the services painted for the Venetians Contarini, Morosini, Pisano-Cornaro and Querini, the name of G. B. Haüer, Hayer, or Hoyer is often associated and one of the few documentary pieces known by this painter is part of a Venetian armorial service. Haüer joined the factory as early as 1724 and by 1731 is recorded as a painter of fine landscapes and figures. There is no reference to arms in the records covering his work, but many of the armorial services are painted with figures in harbour scenes and river landscapes of an unusually vigorous and dramatic type. These are often much more full of contrast than C. F. Herold's harbour scenes; the foregrounds contain dark rocks in silhouette against the lighter landscape backgrounds. Only rarely are armorial wares to be found with coloured grounds.

With Haüer is also associated a series of wares depicting Augustus III and his miners. The minerals of Saxony were a major source of revenue

Right
A large vase with hunting scenes, *c.* 1740, with blue crossed swords mark. A splendid, if not to all eyes beautiful, example of the factory's larger vases at this date. The handles are of a type first modelled by Lucke in the late 1720s. The gilt cartouche shaded in black is typical of this period. The companion vase is still in the Dresden collection.
15 in. high.

70

A hot milk jug and cover, *c.* 1740. Another fine example of the decoration at the end of the decade. The European figures are remarkably freely drawn and colourful.

to the Elector and he showed considerable pride in his miners' activities. The men are shown in their mining uniform, their caps gilt with the A.R. monogram. Later in his career Haüer, who remained at the height of his powers until well into the 1750s, was recorded as one of the best decorators at the factory.

Another able exponent of figure and landscape decoration in this period was J. G. Heintze. He also joined the factory as an apprentice in the mid-1720s and by 1731 was described by J. G. Herold as 'perhaps the best painter'. Many pieces in the vernacular of the period are attributed to him, although they might equally be by C. F. Herold, G. B. Haüer or Johann Christoph Horn, another of the leading decorators. Several landscapes in this style have milestones or signposts, sometimes bearing dates, but more often with more or less illegible cyphers in which some authorities have attempted to read the signatures of one or other of these leading artists, all of whose names, to increase the confusion, begin with the letter H. Perhaps the most reasonable suggestion is that the post-horn which occurs on some of the milestones may be the *Rebus* of

A tea caddy with puce monochrome decoration, *c.* 1740. The square shape shows that this is not a late example. Puce monochrome was used increasingly throughout the 1730s and in the later periods. The vitality of the painting on this piece does not survive in later specimens.

Horn, but even this is only an intelligent supposition. Dated pieces are of course of value since they enable the student to pinpoint more accurately certain types of subject within the period.

The whole question of attribution of decoration to various hands merely serves to highlight how efficient and consistent the Meissen factory was. It emphasises the teamwork which went into the production of the decorated wares, whereby the individual characteristics of even the major artists at the factory were submerged in the gradually changing and evolving decorative style. It leaves a doubt as to whether the continued disputes as to which, if any, of the major artists were responsible for a particular piece, are really meaningful.

The end of the decade saw a gradual movement away from the standard figures in harbour scenes and an expansion of scope in the field of figure and landscape decoration. Pieces are known with panoramic views of the Albrechtsburg and of the city of Dresden. Hunting scenes begin to appear in larger numbers, whilst the actual personages depicted become definitely

European in appearance. In this last trend we may well see the influence
of Kändler at work. For he, not satisfied with the subjects produced by
the decorators, arranged for prints to be sent from France for them to
copy. These were usually after paintings by Watteau or Lancret and
inspired a wide range of scenes of courtly lovers in landscapes. However,
even then the decorators were not entirely dependent on this one group
of prints for inspiration. For the Watteau figures are frequently set in
landscapes with distant castles on hilltops which are derived from a book,
Views in Italy, Friuli and Carinthia, with prints by Melchior Kusel, which
was published in Augsburg in 1681, and which we know was in the factory
library at this date.

Besides Watteau and Lancret another source of inspiration was the
works of the Teniers family, whose paintings provided the source material
for scenes of peasants carousing. From the engravings after Rugendas
came the ideas for battle scenes, which are to be found from 1738 onwards.
Prints of this type by Jeremiah Wolff, J. A. Friedrich and C. Bodenehr
were probably acquired by the factory at the same time as the Watteau
prints.

All these new sources of inspiration did little to revitalise the landscape
and figure decoration at the factory in the later years. The struggle for
supremacy with the modellers ended by reducing the power of the
decorators and placing their work in a subsidiary role to the moulded
shape. Eventually the moulded pieces, too, were to lose their significance
because of this very fact: finely modelled pieces were not successful unless
united with decoration of equivalent standard.

Naturalistic Decoration

The waning of the Chinoiserie decoration and the general loss in prestige suffered by the enamellers in the 1730's was virtually complete in the next decade. Only one sphere still seems to show any vitality, the painting of flowers, fruit and insects.

The development of this theme (described, as we have seen, as *deutsche Blümen* to distinguish it from the stylised Oriental flowers described as

A plate from the Imperial Russian Service, 1741–1745, with crossed swords and impressed '22'. This was modelled by Eberlein for Elizabeth of Russia. The shallow moulding is of the type called *Gotzowsky Erhabene Blumen*. The balance between the brightly coloured but small panels and the larger areas of shallow moulding is very subtle. Many pieces of this service are still in the Hermitage, Leningrad. 9 in. diameter.

A plate with crossed swords mark, 1740–1745, modelled by Eberlein, the central panel painted in copper green with Watteau figures of the type introduced around 1741.
9 in. diameter.

indianische Blümen), reaches well back into the 1730s. It is frequently associated with Johann Gottfried Klinger, a specialist in 'painting coloured flowers' who was at the factory from 1726 to 1746. This type of subject was already well established by about 1735, at which period a large example was supplied to a Venetian client. The flowers were depicted with what can only be described as a stylised naturalism. They were painted with immense precision and brilliance and were made to stand

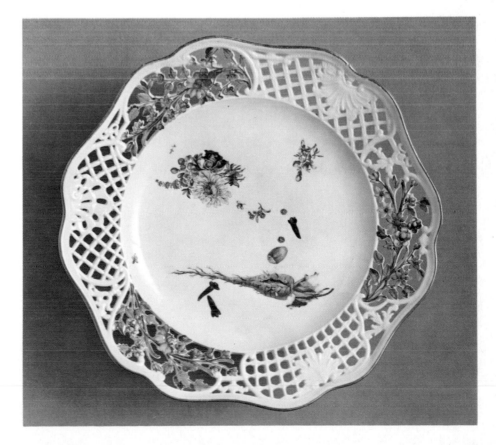

A dessert plate with pierced border, *c.* 1742. Another of the shapes modelled by Eberlein which were to become part of the canon of Meissen, and later European porcelain. This pattern, known as *Brühl'sches Allerlei*, was to be much used at Meissen and Berlin in the 19th century.
9 in. diameter.

A centre dish from the Parnassus Service, *c.* 1745. A very remarkable conception, modelled by Kändler. The somewhat lumpy Muses are typical of his modelling at this date.

A table ornament formed as a cottage, *c.* 1750. Table decorations of this type were modelled for Count Brühl by Eberlein as early as 1742 and they continued in fashion together with tureens formed as fruit and animals.

A hot milk jug, *c.* 1745, with blue crossed swords mark on one foot. These wares with trailing plants in relief were evolved in the 1740s. Specimens of this period are rare, though the concept was endlessly exploited in the last century.

Over page
A lettuce tureen and stand, *c.* 1750, with blue crossed swords mark. Like the cottage, this is a typical rococo conceit, and is one of many tureens modelled as fruit in this period. The model was copied at Chelsea, another prodigious producer of vegetable-shaped tureens.
9 in. diameter.

away from the surface of the plate by very subtle shading. Some pieces are painted with closely detailed botanical specimens derived from books such as the chemist J. W. Weinmann's *Detailed Illustration of a Thousand Plants,* which was published at Regensburg in 1735 and is known to have been used at the factory. However, the majority of the floral pieces of this sort are in fact spuriously botanical and do not depict any particular specimens. The great advantage of this kind of subject was that it was easily adaptable to the plastic shapes that the modellers were evolving. The scattered flower sprays could be spread haphazardly over the moulded surfaces and unlike figure subjects did not require flat spaces to accommodate them.

After Klinger's departure the feeling of the flower decoration changed radically. The forceful, larger-than-life colours of the naturalistic treatment were replaced by softer tones, and the flowers were massed in larger groups instead of the scattered individual specimens of the previous style. The actual flowers, too, are treated much more loosely and superficially and are generally shown as very full blown. Both types of floral painting are found with figure scenes as well.

The interest in natural decoration was not confined to the enamellers. The modellers, too, showed their response to it. Kändler in 1739 modelled vases encrusted with may blossom, a very fussy subject but one which was to be taken up and endlessly repeated, so that, as with Count Brühl's tailor, any pleasure the original conception might have given is diluted by later and inferior interpretations. Of these the vast majority were made at Meissen in the last century, but others were manufactured at Chelsea and Derby whilst Jacob Petit in Paris also made pieces in the idiom. From

A spoon tray, *c.* 1755. The solid ground of previous years was replaced in the 1750s by scale and cell pattern borders such as appear on this piece. The bird painting is a good example in the genre. Other pieces with this decoration are in the Bayerisches Nationalmuseum.

the same period date vases encrusted with climbing vines and other plants, and both tea and dinner wares encrusted with coloured flowers. Groups of fruit and vegetables also began to appear as the finials or handles to tureens and other pieces.

Plant forms even extend to the wares on which the *deutsche Blümen* and other decoration appears. Dishes were modelled as single or overlapping leaves, bowls as lettuce and other leaves, whilst tureens were formed as lemons, roses, oranges, lettuces and other fruit and flowers. Even tea wares occur formed as tulip flowers.

The establishment of new plate forms continued in the 1740s when Eberlein laid down the basic types that Meissen and most other factories have used ever since. The heavily moulded basketwork border of the Sulkowski *ozier* pattern was toned down and combined with lobed or lightly fluted forms, which echo the spiralling shell motif that is the basic shape of the Swan Service. From 1742 come the first of the wares with pierced borders moulded with trailing flower sprays and trellis work, another pattern which was to suffer from endless and mechanical repetition in the 19th century, but which was extremely bold as an original design.

In the 1750s birds joined flowers as one of the staple decorative subjects at the factory. These vary from the single ornithological specimens, culled probably from a book of prints, to groups of brightly coloured birds of no specific species. They are often accompanied by coloured scale or chequer pattern borders in puce, green and pink, and are, perhaps, the last original contribution the factory's enamellers were to make before the Seven Years War was to ruin it financially and deprive it, overnight, of its hegemony among the European porcelain factories.

Figure Modelling after 1740: Kändler, Reinicke, Eberlein

A Gardener, *c.* 1746. Modelled by Eberlein, this figure, with its companion, forms part of the wide range of 'Cris de Paris'-type figures of the 1740s.
7 in. high.

The advent of the Rococo style and the association of Eberlein and Reinicke with Kändler brought about a slight but noticeable change in the feeling of the figures and groups modelled at Meissen. The figures of the 1730s were imbued with a monumentality and a strength which were wholly in accord with their period. They were sufficiently theatrical and arresting to compete for attention with similar creations in other materials. This we saw with the Plât de Mènage. The Rococo style made different requirements of its decorative elements, of which porcelain was a significant one. It required them to fit in and subscribe to a general effect of light, carefree, at times illogical and frequently asymmetrical movement. No longer was the eye to be arrested by a single piece but delighted as it passed over a selection of pieces contributing to an overall effect. The porcelain modeller no longer needed to compete with the sculptor or operate on a grandiose scale that was sometimes better suited to wood, stone or metal. Porcelain figures were increasingly able to establish a scale of their own, while the production of single large figures and groups gave way to series of small figures depicting particular themes.

The exact share in the creative process taken by the various modellers in this period is difficult to unravel. Honey in his *Dresden China* denies any individuality to Reinicke and suggests that Kändler's influence remains paramount. This view would not seem to fit in with the facts. Not merely do the factory's records unequivocally state that Reinicke was the originator of numerous specific models, but the change in style is more marked than could be explained by the gradual change in taste that accompanied the end of the Baroque and the beginning of the Rococo. Also, Kändler's appointment as controller of all the modellers meant that he had less time for creative work on his own. So even when they were working together

the part of the younger man should not be underrated, especially since Reinicke as the younger was probably more in tune with the new spirit.

Kändler had arranged for the supply of prints to the decorators at the factory in 1741. From the same time dates an increasing use of engravings as the source of material for the modellers. These provided the inspiration for some of the most attractive creations of the period.

The first series, quite possibly begun by Kändler, was the *Cris de Paris*, taken from prints by the Comte de Caylus after drawings by Bouchardon. These figures of pancake sellers, a map-seller and others are extremely successful. So, too, are the figures of gardeners modelled at the same time by Eberlein.

Another series, entirely by Kändler, represented miners, similar to those painted by Haüer on the tea-wares. The conception of these is redolent of the previous decade, although they date from around 1748. The black uniforms of the figures contrast strongly with the white porcelain bases and are only relieved by small dashes of other colours. It is probably this that gives them the late Baroque feeling more commonly found in earlier years.

Around 1744 Kändler produced a series of striking Italian Comedy figures in association with Reinicke. Of these the most successful is the Avvocato wearing a voluminous gown, which is found painted bright red, yellow or even left undecorated, and which has a brilliant effect of movement combined with dramatic colouring. These figures are much less monumental in conception than their predecessors.

At the same time Reinicke was working on another extensive series of Italian Comedy figures for the Duke of Weissenfels. These were also

Below

Thirteen Italian Comedy figures. Modelled in 1743–1744 by Reinicke for the Duke of Weissenfels these are derived from François Joulain's prints illustrating Riccoboni's *Histoire du Theatre Italien*, published in Paris in 1728. Here all the major characters of the Italian Comedy are represented: Pulchinello, Pierrot, Pantaloon, Beltrame, Isabella, Columbine, Harlequin, Narcissino, Mezzetin, The Captain, The Doctor, Scapin and Scaramouche. The dominant tones are pink and yellow.

About $5\frac{1}{2}$ in. high.

inspired by prints, the illustrations for Riccoboni's *Histoire du Théâtre Italien* by the engraver Joullain which they followed very closely. The colouring of these figures, which are lighter than those Reinicke modelled with Kändler, is softer and paler. Pink, lilac, yellow and pale green predominate where iron-red, black and a strong yellow had hitherto held sway. They have been criticised as weak when compared with Kändler's earlier figures, but they should be judged by a different yard-stick. They set out to meet a much more lighthearted and less rigorous standard, and as such they should be considered highly successful.

The hand of Reinicke is also to be seen in another series of figures taken from prints, this time de Ferriol's *Différentes Nations du Lévant*. These, depicting Turks, Turkish women and other middle Eastern figures, are again slight but nonetheless very charming. Here once more the paler palette persists, in tune with their unpretentious decorative qualities. It has been suggested that the reliance on prints for inspiration was responsible for the lack of power in these figures, but this may equally well be attributed to the slight shift in taste that had taken place.

The fashion for series of figures grew throughout the decade. Eberlein produced figures of Gods and Goddesses on high, shaped, square bases moulded with emblems in shallow relief. These are extremely sensitive productions which show Eberlein as a considerable master of porcelain modelling. He also created a series of the Seasons, two nymphs and two men on severe square white bases, which show the more robust side of his character.

Kändler, too, was responsible for allegorical figures of Apollo and the Nine Muses. These are less suited to his style of modelling and the nude

A pair of figures of Woodmen, *c.* 1745, modelled by Kändler, probably working with Reinicke. The colouring is still simple, with the white porcelain contributing to the effect.
5¼ in. high.

A figure of a Sportsman, *c.* 1745, modelled
by Kändler.
6 in. high.

figures particularly are sometimes rather lumpy. Other themes which
he depicted were the Continents and a series of figures of tradesmen.
These last, which have the same strength of expression as the miners of
1748, date from around 1750. In 1749 Kändler had visited Paris and had
collected some new ideas. The result of his journey is perhaps to be seen
in the bases of these figures, which are raised, vigorously moulded with
rococo scrolls and enriched with gilding. This new development, perhaps
rather fussy, was to become a permanent feature in the figures and groups
of the 1750s. In about 1752 Kändler and Reinicke modelled another
Cris de Paris series, this time derived from drawings by Huet. These are
slighter than their predecessors and stand on shallow scroll moulded bases.

Eberlein died in 1749, but the resulting gap in the modelling strength
of Meissen was filled by a new figure, F. E. Meyer. He was associated
with Kändler and Reinicke in the creation of the last of the factory's
really beautiful figure groups, again derived from engravings. These were
Chinoiserie groups of ladies and children of great tenderness and delicacy,
taken from J. J. Balechon's engravings of Boucher and entitled *Les Delices
d'Enfance*. (In fact these were not the first Chinoiserie figures at Meissen,
as Kändler had previously produced other single figures of Chinese which,
too, are highly sensitive creations.) Meyer also was responsible for figures
of Malabar musicians which have considerable effect.

Most of the figures and groups modelled at Meissen in the 1750s
were elaborate and depicted purely decorative themes. Shepherds and
Shepherdesses, the archetypal figures of this sort, appeared on the scene
in exaggerated rococo attitudes on scrolling rococo bases. So, too, did
somewhat sentimental family groups of nurses and children, and ladies

A figure of a Peepshowman, *c.* 1753, modelled by Reinicke, perhaps with the collaboration of Kändler after designs by Huet. Notice the moulded and gilt wave scrolls, introduced a few years earlier. 5¼ in. high.

sewing and spinning. The decorative complexity of these creations does not compensate for their comparative lack of sculptural qualities. Kändler's creative force seems stifled by the trivial movement of the Rococo, and it may be of course that his direct involvement with the modelling process had diminished. In 1749 he had been promoted to *Hofkommisar* and no doubt this too had increased his administrative commitments. Furthermore, the vast number of employees at the factory included many lesser modellers working in the master's style and to whom much of this later work, although prepared under his supervision and even following his suggestions, must be more directly attributed.

The 1740s and 1750s are undoubtedly dominated by Kändler, but this was a period where the change in feeling which he had initiated was as strongly expressed by the men working with and under him. Unfortunately, the advent of the Rococo which found Nymphenburg and Höchst in the full force of their opening years, came to Meissen after another style had already been successfully established. Thus this period, when compared with the 1730s and despite the immense commercial success that factory enjoyed, does not show the same distinction.

Right
A group of Chinese Lovers in an Arbour, *c.* 1750, probably modelled by Reinicke. This is an outstanding example of the Rococo at Meissen.

Left
A figure of a Turkish Woman in an Arbour,
c. 1750. Modelled by Reinicke, this and
many similar figures were derived from
illustrations to Ferriols' *Receuil de Cent
Estampes Representant Differentes Nations du
Levant.*

Above
A group of a beggarwoman and children—
from the Kandler workshop—circa 1750;
the colouring of this example is peculiarly
felicitous and subtle, showing a deep understanding of porcelain as a material.

Small Boxes and Other Products

Throughout the 18th century at Meissen, besides the figures and table wares, there was continuous production of boxes, pipeheads and other small *Galanterie* objects. These, whilst reflecting the general trends of the other items produced at the factory are of great use to the student. For although the majority of pieces of this sort bear no factory marks, the incidence of signatures and other means of definite identification is much greater.

Owing to the fact that boxes were often used for presentation by Augustus the Strong and other monarchs, they can frequently be dated very closely. Furthermore the expensive mounts, often gold or silver gilt, with which they were fitted, encouraged the porcelain manufacturers to produce pieces worthy of them. As a result the best decorators were often responsible for their decoration, and, out of pride for their finest work, they would occasionally include a signature, albeit cryptic, in the decoration.

Another feature of boxes is that each is complete in itself. The decoration does not have to match that on other pieces in the same set. Therefore, as well as being the vehicle for the factory's most proficient painting, the porcelain box at Meissen also constituted the field for some of its most adventurous decoration.

The early boxes of the 1720s were, like the contemporary tea wares and vases, very plain in shape, generally oval but of varying depth. The surfaces, as on the other wares, were either flat or curved but with no moulded decoration, affording the best scope for the activities of the enamellers. (Many of the boxes of this date bear the K.P.M. mark painted on the inside.) The more ordinary examples are decorated with the same Chinoiserie scenes that are the hallmark of the contemporary wares. Others, particularly those that were Royal gifts or made for Royal use, bear more elaborate and original decoration.

The 1730s witnessed a far larger production of boxes. The development of painted and plastic decoration imparted a variety to the manufacture. As on the wares, the Chinoiserie figures gave way to harbour scenes and these were very frequently accompanied by coloured grounds. The shape also underwent a significant change, becoming slightly bombé and shell shaped. The Kakiemon style, too, is found very occasionally on snuff-boxes, with playing boys painted in the manner attributed to Löwenfinck.

The advent of surface moulding in the late 1730s greatly enlarged the scope of box production. As a result the box provided an opportunity for both aspects of Meissen production to flourish in harmony. The exterior, which is vulnerable to rubbing and therefore ill-suited to enamelled decoration, was given over to the modellers to display their talents, whilst the interior of the lid, and sometimes the whole inside, was the domain of the decorator. The effects of this combination are remarkable. Frequently the exterior of Meissen boxes in this period is entirely white, relying solely on the restraint of basketwork or, around the time of the Swan Service, on vigorous scrolls beautifully set off by the golden metal of the hinge mounts. Opening the box will often reveal the decorators' work in the best miniaturist style, perhaps using stippling with great skill because

Above right
A lilac ground box, *c.* 1735, of the bombé shape often found in the mid-1730s and decorated with the usual Middle Eastern merchants in harbour scenes.

A deep oval box with a classical subject in puce monochrome, 1740–1745. This shape, more common in the 1720s, is unusual in the later period, but particularly well suited to this type of all-round decoration.
2½ in. wide.

Below right
A Chinoiserie shallow oval box, *c.* 1725. A rare shape offering rather inconvenient and limited space for the decorator. This perhaps explains the small number to be found.
2½ in. wide.

A Chinoiserie deep oval box, *c.* 1725. This is the classic shape of the 1720s. Frequently the 'K.P.M.' mark is found inside. The shape offers a good surface for the decorator.
2½ in. wide.

A box painted by J. G. Herold, *c.* 1735. The scene of Danäe receiving the shower of

92

they could be confident that, inside the lid, their work would be well protected.

C. F. Herold was active throughout the 1730s in box decoration, and signed examples of his work are known. So, too, are pieces signed by two other able exponents of miniature painting on boxes, both active in the 1740s and 1750s–J. M. Heinrici and J. G. Wagner. Both these men are more usually described as the leading decorators of the 1750s but a recently discovered signed and dated piece by Wagner shows that even in

gold, which appears on the inside of the lid, is after the painting by Titian and bears Herold's signature. As is often the case with the inside panels of box lids this is painted in a stippled technique such as is used by miniaturists. The protection afforded by the box encouraged the decorators to produce their best work inside the lid. The exterior of this box shows the later Chinoiserie decoration at its most brilliant.

the early 1740s his technical and artistic skills were already highly developed. Wagner only arrived at Meissen in 1739, and was taken on as a miniature painter. In 1741, or perhaps early 1742, he was responsible for the remarkable box illustrated. This depicts the major events of the first nine months of the First Silesian War, in which Frederick the Great of Prussia attacked and defeated the Austrians, gaining the valuable province

A documentary royal presentation snuff-box. signed 'Johann Georg Wagner 1741' but probably not executed until the following year. This hitherto unpublished box commemorates the successful 1741 campaign of Frederick the Great in the First Silesian War. The cover shows the King (on a white horse to the left) before the city of Niesse in April of that year. The siege was noted for Frederick's use of flaming mortars, clearly depicted here by the artist. The remaining surfaces of the exterior show other incidents of the campaign and the interior of the cover shows the Arts acknowledging the triumph of Prussia. It is interesting that this major example of the factory's production should have been commissioned by Frederick at this date.
4 in. diameter.

Four scent bottles, c. 1725: variations on the earliest form found in porcelain, with harbour scenes and Chinoiseries.
About 2½ in. high.

Three boxes depicting the factory's great patrons.

Centre
A royal presentation box, *c.* 1730. The portrait inside the cover is that of Augustus the Strong, while the Royal Arms of Saxony appear on the front. On the outside of the cover is Augustus' monogram. This was evidently made either for Augustus' personal use or as a gift from him. The decoration has been attributed to J. G. Herold.
2¾ in. wide.

Below
A pair of portrait boxes, *c.* 1738, painted with portraits of Count Brühl and his wife Franciska von Kolowrat-Krakowska.

of Silesia. The exterior of the box, portraying the military events of the war, is painted in a bold style which displays considerable mastery, whilst the inside of the cover, depicting the Arts and Sciences paying homage to Prussia, is an outstanding example of stipple technique. A comparison of this box with others produced in the 1740s may eventually enable further examples to be added to the established canon of Wagners work.

Heinrici came to Meissen two years after Wagner in 1741. As well as snuff-boxes, he was noted for portraiture and was also an expert in colours. Among his signed works is a portrait plaque of Augustus III, although this, despite the technical proficiency displayed, is rather severe and looks forward to the prolific production of porcelain plaques throughout Germany in the 19th century.

The snuff-box was not unaffected by the animal modelling of Kändler, and examples were made in this genre. So too were pipe heads, scent bottles and cane handles. Scent bottles in the 1720s were shaped like pilgrim flasks, a form found in Oriental porcelain, European pottery

Left
A snuff-box formed as a seated Turk, *c.* 1745. The model for this comes from the Kändler/Reinicke circle.
4½ in. high.

Above
Left
A snuff-box with a recumbent pug dog, *c.* 1740. One of Kändler's delightful interpretations of this theme put to a practical use. The inside of the cover carries a still life subject.

Centre
An oval box, *c.* 1738. The shallow moulding of the exterior, almost certainly by Kändler, echoes that of the Swan Service. A series of boxes of this type was made for the Brühl family.

Right
A pipe head formed as a pug dog, 1740–1745. The hinged head has pierced ears to let in the air and the stem of the pipe fits beneath the tail. This is a typical 'conceit' of the period.

Opposite page
Above left
A circular snuff-box, *c.* 1740. These fine large boxes show some of the best of the factory's work when the decoration of the wares had already lost it originality. With three good surfaces, uninterrupted by moulding, they are usually attributable to one of the leading decorators and show how imaginative the painters remained. The dark figures in the foreground are often regarded as the hallmark of Haüer.
4 in. diameter.

Above right
A cylindrical box and cover in the Kakiemon style, *c.* 1735. Kakiemon decoration on small wares is fairly uncommon. This piece was probably made for a dressing table with matching tapersticks and fan-shaped boxes.
3½ in diameter.

Below left
A circular moulded box, *c.* 1740. Here the moulded white exterior is relieved only by the insects in the centre, but the box opens to reveal a brilliantly painted scene inside the cover.
4 in. diameter.

Below right
A grisaille circular box, *c.* 1745. This shows strongly the influence of the French engravings brought from Paris in 1741. The decoration is much less powerful than that on the harbour scene box of five years earlier.
3½ in. diameter.

and silver. The flattened bodies provided another good surface for the decorators of the period to display their skill.

In the 1730s the advent of figure modelling introduced a new dimension to the category of wares, and an extensive production of miniature figures, birds and animals, often reductions of the larger models, took place. Some of these were quite easily adapted into scent bottles by modelling the head separately and attaching them to the bodies by metal mounts. Meissen porcelain was also used for watches, where the face and the back were of porcelain. Another highly original product of the factory was chess sets, complete with porcelain boards and the places for the pieces painted with suitable figures.

The attire of the smart gentleman was not complete without a snuff-box and a watch of Meissen porcelain in his waistcoat pockets. His cane also required a porcelain handle, and these, too, the factory supplied in profusion. Some were of plain knob form, but many more were T-shaped with the crosspiece slightly scrolled. Frequently these were comparatively plain with painted decoration. Others, as with snuff-boxes, are a happy combination of the modellers' and decorators' skills, having one end formed as an animal or figurehead in the manner of Kändler and the other decorated with Watteau scenes or other subjects.

All these small bibelots display the versatility and commercial enterprise of Meissen at the height of the factory's success. They show how the porcelain manufacturers had invaded what had hitherto been the preserve of the silver-smith, and had established their own material as a serious competitor to gold, silver, hardstone and other materials. In this Meissen once again set an example that was to be followed very quickly

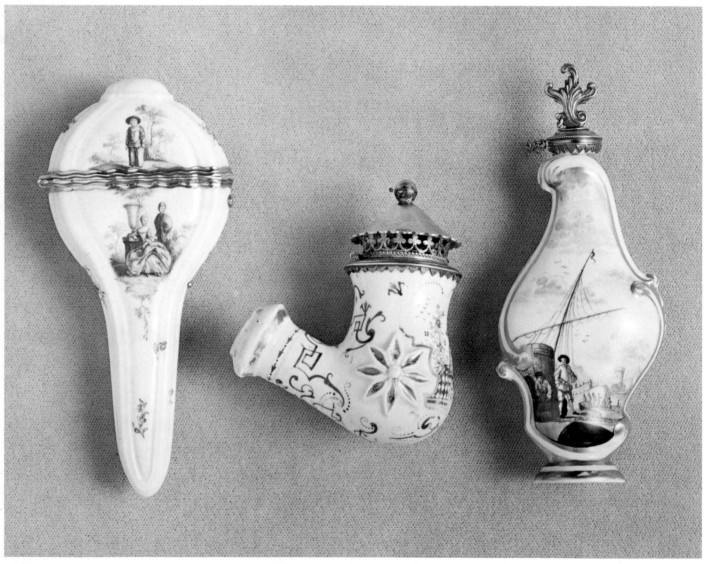

by other factories throughout Europe. So great, in fact, was the production of scent bottles at Chelsea in the 1750s, that it affected the market for Meissen's output significantly, just at the time of the factory's greatest difficulties.

Although not often such imposing works of art as the factory's larger and more monumental products, these small pieces produced at Meissen were yet another of its serious contributions to the development of porcelain production in Europe.

Decoration Outside the Factory

Above left

A pair of knife and fork handles, 1730–1735
The brilliant decoration on these shows the
minute attention to detail and the consistency of quality that permeated the
factory's activities in every sphere.

Below left

A scissors case, c. 1745.
An early pipe head, c. 1725.
A rococo scent bottle, c. 1745.

The scent bottle is a typical example of the
1740s. The form with its scrolled edges is
essentially rococo. The pipe head has all
the features of the early Herold period,
Chinoiseries and *Laub-und-Bandelwerk*. The
monochrome decoration on the scissors
case shows the direct influence of the
prints after Watteau acquired by the
factory in 1741. The standing figure on
the cover is derived from a print of
Watteau's most famous painting, Gilles,
in the Louvre.

From the early 1720s there was an increasing quantity of Meissen porcelain that was decorated outside the factory. The uncertainty of the firing
process in the early years resulted in a fairly high proportion of 'wasters'
which were sold off to outside decorators, commonly known as *Hausmalers*.
These men, operating in Dresden, Augsberg, Breslau, Pressnitz, Bayreuth
and even in Holland, were responsible for a wide variety of decoration
which, whilst frequently of high quality and originality, was to prove
more and more of an embarrassment and nuisance to the factory itself.
This eventually was to result in a situation tantamount to war between
the factory and the *Hausmalers*, but the resultant pieces are an important
aspect of the history of decoration on European porcelain.

The *Hausmaler* was not a new phenomenon which appeared with the
discovery of European porcelain. Outside decoration in cold enamels had
already been extensively practised at Bayreuth, where the local faience
and glass from nearby Bohemia was decorated by the Preissler family.
Nor indeed were the attentions of the *Hausmaler* limited to Meissen. They
were equally applied to early Vienna wares and to Chinese porcelain.

The early *Hausmaler* decoration around Dresden was mostly in unfired
enamel colours which were markedly inferior to those used at Meissen.
The resultant products caused great annoyance to the factory and in
order to distinguish the wares decorated in the factory from those outside
pieces, the first marks were introduced in 1723. Unfortunately the inferior cold enamels were not very durable and rubbed or flaked off only
too easily and therefore comparatively few pieces of this sort have survived.
There are few names known and the most identifiable figure would seem
to be Lauch, or Lauche, a decorator who was employed first at Meissen
and then set up on his own in Dresden. His work, of which signed examples
exist, is generally a crude travesty of the Chinoiserie decoration he had
used at the factory, executed in makeshift colours since the refined ones
employed at Meissen were not available to him. These comments could
easily be applied to most Dresden *Hausmalers*, but Lauch's work compared
well with the work produced in other centres by decorators who had
more efficient firing facilities.

The most extensive class of early *Hausmalerei* wares was decorated in
Augsburg, where there was a thriving industry in silver and gold and from
whence came the mounts for any major pieces of Meissen. Here there
were two highly successful decorating shops, operated by the Seuter and
Auffenwerth families.

Abraham and Bartolomaus Seuter decorated both white and blue and
white Meissen porcelain with gilt Chinoiserie scenes. These were very
finely engraved and show a marked affinity with contemporary Meissen

A tankard with goldchinese decoration, *c.* 1730, the silver gilt mounts by Elias Adam, Augsburg. An unusually well preserved example of the Seuter family's most famous type of decoration. So often the gilt is rubbed and loses some of the delicate engraving with which the detail is brought out.
7 in. high.

Chinoiserie decoration in Herold's studio. So much do some of the subjects echo those enamelled on factory decorated pieces, that it was quite recently believed by some authorities that *goldchinese* decoration was done at Meissen itself. Pazaurek's revolutionary work on *Hausmaler* decoration, published in 1925 and the bible of this subject, whilst discussing several pieces of faience from the Seuter workshop, docs not ascribe any *goldchinese* decoration to his family, although one or two pieces illustrated by him and ascribed to Auffenwerth at Augsburg should now probably be reattributed to the Seuter family. This same confusion persisted when W. B. Honey discussed the subject in *Dresden China* in 1934, and the whole question was only clarified in 1966/67 by Drs S. Ducret and A. Torré who identified Bartolomaus Seuters signature on a piece with *goldchinese* decoration. This formed part of a complete travelling tea and coffee service, which could thus all be confidently attributed to Seuter and provided a basis for comparison with other pieces. At the same time it was noticed that an engraved portrait of Seuter showed examples of his products on a shelf behind him. These, too, are unmis-

A Dresden *Hausmalerei* teapot, *c.* 1725. This bears the signature of the *Hausmaler* Lauche. The bilious green he used is a good sign that it is an outside decorated piece as the green used at Meissen was a closely guarded secret. The actual painting is also less skilful than that on factory decorated wares or even on pieces painted by Auffenwerth in Augsburg.
7 in. high.

Below
A Böttger teapot with Augsburg enamelled decoration, also from the Seuter workshop: this is an example of their enamelled decoration of European genre scenes.

A Böttger teabowl and saucer with Augsburg *goldchinese* decoration: this well illustrates its characteristic subtlety.

takenly examples of *goldchinese* decoration. Since then a large group of *goldchinese* wares, decorated over white and blue and white and derived by descent from the Saxon Royal Family, has appeared on the market and provided yet another opportunity for a study in depth of this workshop. The similarity of some of the designs to those of Herold's Chinoiseries is explained by the fact that Seuter did work under Herold at one stage, and it is probable that the relationship between the factory and this particular outside decorating shop was fairly friendly.

Johann Auffenwerth, the other major Augsburg *Hausmaler* to whom the mass of Augsburg decoration on Meissen porcelain was attributed, was far less difficult to pinpoint. For, whereas Seuter's signature was cryptically concealed on a small tablet held by a Chinaman on one of his pieces, Auffenwerth painted his initials, and even the date, quite clearly on some of his wares. This made it very much simpler to attribute other unsigned pieces to his workshop, in which he was assisted, and succeeded on his death in 1728, by his daughter Sabina. He specialised in decoration in iron-red, black and silver of genre scenes within scroll cartouches not

A Chinoiserie teabowl and saucer decorated at Augsburg. The feathery lightness of these Chinoiseries is characteristic of Johann Auffenwerth and should be compared with the rather more robust work of the factory itself at this time.

dissimilar from those used at the factory. However, he covered the remaining surface with formal scroll work which was in the contemporary fashion, but in a manner entirely peculiar to himself.

Besides the wares that fall specifically into the œuvre of either Seuter or Auffenwerth there are many others which were undoubtedly decorated in Augsburg, and which might derive from either workshop or another that has not yet been identified. Notable among these are hunting and battle subjects, decorated either in silver or gold in a technique similar to *goldchinese*, which have been attributed to Auffenwerth but might equally originate from the Seuter workshop. Another distinctive group is of coloured Chinoiseries, similar to those painted in the factory but perhaps more sketchy, and accompanied by light and feathery gilt *Laub-und-Bandelwerk*. It is tempting to see in these the production of Auffenwerth's studio after his death.

After Dresden and Augsburg, the next major centre of *Hausmalerei* was Breslau. Here again in the 1720s two major decorating establishments were operating, those of Ignaz Bottengruber and Ignaz Preissler, two of

103

A Böttger bowl with Bayreuth *Hausmaler* decoration, the bowl *c.* 1720, the decoration a few years later. This outstanding example of Chinoiserie painting is probably the work of the *Hausmaler* Dannhofer, though some authorities see in it the work of the young J. G. Herold at Meissen itself. The bowl is somewhat misshapen and therefore outside decoration is rather more likely.
6¾ in. diameter.

A teabowl and saucer with Callot scenes, *c.* 1725. Only three teabowls and saucers are recorded with this fine and amusing decoration. This too was probably painted at Bayreuth and has been attributed to Dannhofer. Whoever the decorator, there can be no doubt as to his ability.

the greatest masters of porcelain decoration. Until Pazaurek devoted himself to the whole question of *Hausmaler* decoration on German porcelain and faience, 'Bottengruber' was used as a generic term to describe all *Hausmalerei* decoration.

Ignaz Bottengruber was established as a miniature painter and water-colourist before he took to decorating porcelain (he also went in for book illustration and, later in his career, painted Boucher-type scenes on ivory). However, his activity as a *Hausmaler* dates from the very early 1720s and he worked not only on Meissen but on the two other forms of porcelain available to him, Chinese and Viennese porcelain. He drew his ideas from prints, and from the decorating style already established on glass and faience by his fellow citizens, the Preisslers.

Many of his pieces are decorated in iron-red and purple monochrome with scenes of Gods and Goddesses feasting, derived from prints by J. T. de Bry. In 1725 he produced a service painted with panels of animals of the chase. Later in the decade and in the early 1730s he decorated in a more forceful and individual late Baroque style. This included human and animal grotesque decoration with very rich Baroque foliage, and mythological scenes enclosed by extremely elaborate *Laub-und-Bandelwerk* containing birds, masks and other features.

The number of signed examples of his work is unusually high and many of these are dated, enabling a close assessment of the development of his style to be made. The frequent appearance of his signature makes it quite clear that Bottengruber regarded painting on porcelain as the equal of painting on any other material. It is often more simple to identify Bottengruber's work than the porcelain on which it appears, because the similarity between Meissen and early Vienna porcelain, which was derived from it, is very great.

Ignaz Preissler came of a family of glass and pottery decorators which had been established in Nuremburg in the 17th century. They had evolved a tradition of monochrome decoration on these materials, and there were several other decorators working in the style whom, like Bottengruber, used Chinese porcelain. Monochrome was still used on porcelain, but in a much lighter vein than in Bottengruber's pieces. The formal grotesque decoration, which reflects the contemporary Règence taste for foliage and strapwork, is spread in a feathery network all over the surface of the porcelain. This class of decoration is usually in black monochrome, or *schwarzlot* as it is commonly known. In iron-red monochrome are found pieces with figures in extensive landscapes, depicting subjects such as Abraham sacrificing Isaac and other religious scenes.

In the late 1730s in Bayreuth another *Hausmaler* had an active workshop, J. F. Metsch. Much of the porcelain he decorated dated from the early 1720s, and came equally from Vienna and Meissen. His decoration included still life subjects and landscapes in shaped strapwork cartouches of a very conservative variety. He also painted Chinoiserie scenes in the style of Herold, but the distinctive cartouches that occur with this type of decoration make these easily identifiable.

In Pressnitz another decorator, F. J. Mayer, was the head of a further workshop during the same period. Once again, the porcelain he used was often early Meissen. However, the European figures that are the dominant feature show that they date from the 1740s, and his scenes are often bordered by shaped line cartouches. Many more plates in his manner are found than in the case of the other decorators.

European figures are a distinguishing characteristic of another of the later *Hausmalers*, F. J. Ferner. He also worked in the 1740s and, unlike the majority of *Hausmalers*, decorated mainly on the lightly fluted blue and white tea wares which were among the cheaper types that Meissen produced. These he painted with European figure subjects, many of them set in peasant scenes. His style is much less sophisticated than that of Metsch or Mayer. Perhaps the most unusual decorative technique was that used in the 1750s by Canon August Otto von dem Busch of Hildesheim. He engraved white porcelain with flowers and figure and animal scenes

Above

Three Meissen sugar bowls and covers. The two oval examples are typical of the early 1720s, the circular bowl is not a common shape and probably dates from around 1728. The plain oval shape is frequently found with a silver gilt hinge. The decoration is: *left* iron red mono-chrome, *centre* enamelled in Holland, *right* a still-life subject by J. F. Metzch. The Dutch decorating shops, which used Chinese porcelain, Meissen and, later in the century, English creamware, used very hard enamels which stand away from the surface of the porcelain and in which iron red is a prominent feature. The coffee pot from this service is in the Victoria and Albert Museum. Metzch's decoration was of a very high standard and the piece shown here is a good specimen of his work.

A plate painted by Mayer of Pressnitz. An example of Mayer's most usual manner. 9 in. diameter.

An octagonal bottle-shaped vase with
Dutch decoration. This *famille rose* palette
is the other dominant type in Dutch
enamelling on Meissen. This vase was
evidently intended for decoration at the
factory in the Kakiemon style.

A Meissen blue and white bowl painted by
J. P. Ferner. Here a simple Meissen bowl
with underglaze blue painting in the
Oriental style has been overpainted in
iron red, green, brown and yellow with
figures which were not in the original
design.
7 in. diameter.

Two cream pots, the porcelain *c.* 1725.

Left
The blue and white decoration is by the factory painter Kretschmar, the red and gold overpainting perhaps by an outside decorator.

Right
This is painted in iron red and black with the Sacrifice of Abraham by Ignaz Preissler at Breslau. The scene occupies the entire surface of the body and demonstrates Preissler's skill as a landscape painter. The cover is painted with the *Laub-und-Bandelwerk* with which he is usually associated.

A hexagonal tea caddy and cover, the porcelain, *c.* 1725, with iron red monochrome decoration possibly by Melhorn in Dresden.

A teabowl and saucer with landscape scenes, the porcelain 1725–1730, probably decorated by a Dresden *Hausmaler*.

A large dish with engraved decoration by Canon von dem Busch, *c.* 1755. 13 in. diameter.

which were then filled in black. It is an interesting and original technique, but was too laborious to endure.

By the 1750s the numerous factories that were starting up all over Germany put an end to the market for the *Hausmalers'* wares. Hitherto the only means of obtaining porcelain decorated in any style other than that produced by the factory artists had been the *Hausmaler*. Now a greater variety was offered and the need that the independent decorator fulfilled had disappeared. (Naturally there are many *Hausmalers* who have not been positively identified and the subject still offers wide scope for research. Many quite competently enamelled pieces are to be found which do not fit into the style of the decorators we have discussed, but unless documentary pieces come to light it is difficult to make any definite attributions.)

The whole body of *Hausmalerei* decoration is an interesting and important aspect of the development of enamelled and other decoration on porcelain in Europe. The outside decorators provided a series of different solutions to the question of enamelling porcelain, which gave alternatives to those offered at Meissen and contributed to the more varied types of decoration which appeared in the second and third quarters of the century.

Above
A *Hausmaler* teapot with battle scenes, the porcelain *c.* 1723, the decoration probably Dresden *c.* 1730. This, like many evidently outside decorated pieces, is difficult to ascribe to a particular hand.
7 in. wide.

Meissen after
the Seven Years War

The economic catastrophe of the Seven Years War, which left Saxony crushed by Frederick the Great, saw many of the workmen, among them F. E. Meyer, removed to Berlin from Meissen. Simultaneously the full effect of the competition from Sèvres, which was enjoying the full patronage of Louis XV, began to make itself felt. The new style of rich coloured grounds, far more brilliant than could ever be made on the hard-paste porcelain at Meissen, swept the entire porcelain-making world, but it was better suited to the soft-paste manufacturers of England and France than the weakened Meissen factory bankrupt of inspiration and resources. At the same time the small factories all over Germany, which were perhaps more attuned to the new style, were providing competition.

In the face of these mounting difficulties Meissen had relatively little to offer. Many of the old models, so successfully established in the 1730s and 1740s, continued in production. Often they can only be distinguished superficially from their predecessors by the decoration, which is less simple and tends to extend to the bases, hitherto white or partly gilt. There were of course active modellers such as C. G. Punct and M. Acier. The former died in 1765, but Acier, who arrived from Paris in 1764, remained at or attached to the factory until his death in 1799. Kändler, too, remained working at Meissen until his own death in 1775, but apart from the modelling of a few special commissions his contribution was probably not very significant.

To Acier must be ascribed almost all the factory's original work in this era. From his hand came the increasingly austere and neo-classical groups of children emblematic of the Seasons, the Arts, and other allegorical themes. In these the Rococo scroll base is replaced by a circular base edged with flutes. On these models the decoration is much more diffuse than that of earlier periods. The palette used relies heavily on purples, browns, pale yellows and other sober colours, and these are spread over all the surfaces in a much less controlled fashion than before. As a result, perhaps, the plastic pieces of this period are not very striking in effect.

A tureen cover and stand, *c.* 1770, with blue crossed swords and dot mark. The shape and the putto surmounting the cover are typical of table wares of this date. The almost neo-classical floral painting, rather spiritless when compared with that of previous periods, is another characteristic feature.

The same criticism may be equally levelled against the wares. These continued to adhere to the established shapes laid down in the 1740s and there was a considerable production of table wares. The main trouble springs from the transplanting of Sèvres patterns and ideas, intended for the subtle surface of soft-paste porcelain, which produces a somewhat stark effect on the true porcelain of Meissen. Thus, although there was no lack of production, the decoration is usually unexciting; cut fruit, flowers, birds and other patterns which were the stock-in-trade of every porcelain factory of the day. Hitherto at Meissen the decoration had thrived on innovation and in setting an example to others. Now it merely formed a part of the general mainstream of porcelain decoration and even that in a secondary role.

When in 1780 Count Camillo Marcolini took over the administration of the factory, a situation which was to last to the end of the century, the products at Meissen moved still further into the cold atmosphere of neo-classicism. This was even less well suited to porcelain as a decorative material. Plain shapes and severe decoration were to be found all over Europe at this time, an era when porcelain was less adapted to current fashion than in the previous great periods of Baroque and Rococo of which it had been a salient exponent. At Meissen the products were no exception to the general trend and the factory was forced to take its ideas from other manufacturers.

Many pieces were decorated with medallions, swags and reliefs in what is called in England the Adam Style. The landscape decoration which had always been a staple feature of the factory's output, and which was also to be found on the wares of its German competitors, persisted. How-

A group of Cherry Pickers, *c.* 1766, with blue crossed swords and dot mark. One of Kändler's last models, after a print of a painting by Boucher. Note the gilt rocaille base.
7½ in. high.

ever, it is more monotonous and less brilliantly executed than in previous years.

The factory at Sèvres had made a very successful range of groups in unglazed white porcelain or 'biscuit'. This type was adopted at Meissen, as at Vienna and Derby. Unfortunately, as with the coloured decoration derived from Sèvres, the white of hard-paste biscuit is far harsher and æsthetically less pleasing than its soft-paste equivalent, and the products

A group of children emblematic of Fire from a set of the Elements, *c.* 1770. The rather more general use of colour, which smothers the white of the porcelain, looks forward to later developments. The high pierced base, a typical late rococo feature, is to be found on most groups made throughout Europe at this date.
$5\frac{1}{2}$ in. high.

of Sèvres and Derby are more attractive than anything produced in this material at Meissen.

Sèvres was not the sole influence that made itself felt in Meissen. The blue and white jasper wares of Josiah Wedgwood were imitated in France and at Meissen.

The transition from the Punct period to the Marcolini was not, of course, a sharp one, but a gradual process as in any trend in style. In the 1760s and 1770s the pieces were marked with a dot between the crossed swords. In the 1780s the dot was replaced by a star, but even this was a gradual change and many services are to be found containing pieces bearing both types of mark.

The changes in figures and groups was no more sensible. Their significant characteristic now was the absence of any great plastic expression, and they are generally allegorical or purely decorative. The urge to compete with sculpture, which had inspired the early subjects, had died a gradual death, while their production, which had developed the factory's technical skill to a high level, persisted long after creative innovation had ceased and could not make up for the lack of inspiration.

19th Century Production

The creative success of the Meissen factory in its early years was a limiting factor in its development in the second half of the 18th century. This process was even more marked in the 19th century, when, for the most part, the shapes, models and to some extent the decoration of the mid-18th century continued in unimaginative use, as indeed they do to this day.

Naturally the production was influenced considerably by contemporary taste, and the use made of 18th century models forms an interesting commentary on 19th century fashion. Many of the models that were repeated were comparatively rare in their original editions, and are much more in tune with the later period. Typical of these are the vast body of wares and vases encrusted with may blossom and other flowers, models originally evolved by Kändler in the 1740s. These are not merely more common in the later period, but are imbued with all the elaboration and vulgarity which is by many associated with the Victorian era. Other vases, often of massive proportions, are modelled with cupids, fruit and flowers and decorated with figures in landscapes, the elaborate covers surmounted by sprays of flowers and pierced and moulded with coloured scrolls.

The dinner wares continue in the use of the shapes established by Eberlein, with ozier borders or moulded with spiral flutes. The decoration, whether of European or Oriental flowers, is mechanical and lifeless when compared with that of the best period.

The production of blue and white wares had never proved very successful in the 18th century, though examples are to be found. Despite this, the prolific output of blue and white wares in the 19th century was focused on an undoubtedly 18th century prototype, the 'onion pattern'.

Figure modelling drew equally deeply on the ideas of the previous century, but the emphasis, as in the Punct and Marcolini periods, is on the purely decorative or slightly allegorical, rather than on the Harlequins and Oriental or Polish figures which are among the most exciting late Baroque or Rococo models. The crinoline groups, however, are frequently repeated, appealing as they did almost more to 19th century taste than they do today. Unfortunately these, above all, suffered from the fact that the originals were decorated under the close supervision of their creator, Kändler, and the enamellers were firmly controlled. The decoration of the same models in the 19th century was less well-regulated and not often in keeping with the spirit of the originals. Instead of the broad masses of

116

A group of ladies, c. 1840. A late example after the original model by Acier. The colours, which are slightly harsh, and the colour of the porcelain itself, combined with a large mark and incised shape number on the base all show that this is a late piece.
9½ in. high.

A group of the Spanish Lovers, late 19th century, after the original model illustrated on page 59. The decoration used detracts from the effect of the group, where on the original it added to it.
8 in. high.

A figure of a Jay, mid-19th century. A version of the model by Kändler of 1739–1740. The all-pervasive decoration with its rather shiny surface should be compared with the earlier example illustrated on page 58.
15 in. high.

colour used with such effect by the Baroque enamellers, there was a more diffuse and fussy use of floral decoration, and where in the original interpretations the bases had been left plain, the decorators covered even these with colour, thus diminishing the impact of the modelling.

The same fate overtook the animal figures. The forceful and brilliant technique of the 18th century was replaced by a smoother and more monotonous treatment. This, too, embraced the tree stumps, hitherto left white and setting off the bright plumage of the birds, and much reduced the general effect.

Not all the productions of the 19th century were repetitions of 18th century ideas, although those that were original were hardly more fortunate. Besides the encrusted vases after early models, there were numerous mirrors, candelabra, girandoles and centre pieces encrusted with flowers, birds and cupids which were remarkably fine in execution although suffering from the tendency to over-elaborate which is typical of the period.

Had the factory not leaned so heavily on the ideas of the previous

A vase of flowers, *c.* 1850. This is a rococo model, found very rarely in its original 18th century form, but fairly common in the 19th century. The combination of pink, turquoise and gilding is a standard feature of the period.

century, it is unlikely in fact that it would have produced anything more significant. This was an era in which porcelain as a material and an art form suffered seriously from the effects of mass production and the suppression of originality which this brought with it. This, in fact, was the eventual result of the methods of production which the factory had established from the outset, methods which were extremely modern in their original conception but which eventually considerably diminished the will to invent which is a necessary source of progress and change.